Kentucky
FOOTNOTES

BYRON CRAWFORD

foreword by ERIC CRAWFORD

Acclaim Press
MORLEY, MISSOURI

Acclaim Press
— Your Next Great Book —
P.O. Box 238
Morley, MO 63767
(573) 472-9800
www.acclaimpress.com

Story and photo research: Amy Inskeep
Layout design: Emily Sikes
Cover design: M. Frene Melton
Managing Editor: Randy Baumgardner
Proofreader: Steve Russell
Original Courier-Journal copy editors: Charlie Archer, Joe Baldwin, Judy Bryant,
    Carla Carlton, Rob Deckard, Harold Freeman, Nick Hollkamp, Tiffany Meredith,
    Glenn Nesmith, Glenn Ow, Steve Russell, Rich Schiefer, Wayne Wells, Alan
    Wild, Carolyn Yetter.
Original Courier-Journal photo editors: Cindy Stucky, Bill Luster, Kim Kolarik,
    Marcella Johnson, Pat McDonogh, Mary Ann Gerth.
Archival photo reproduction: Harry King, Valynda Tindle
Art: Herman Wiederwohl, Byron Crawford
Cover photo: Tim Thornberry
Author photo: Greg Biagi

Library of Congress Cataloging-in-Publication Data

Crawford, Byron.
  Kentucky footnotes / by Byron Crawford.
    p. cm.
  Summary: Collection of the author's columns originally published by The
Louisville Courier-Journal.
  ISBN-13: 978-1-935001-30-0 (alk. paper)
  ISBN-10: 1-935001-30-2 (alk. paper)
  1. Kentucky--Social life and customs. I. Title.
  F456.2.C725 2009
  976.9--dc22
                          2009039856

First Printing: 2010
Printed in the United States of America
10 9 8 7 6 5 4 3 2 1

Contents

Dedication

TO my parents, Delbert and Lucille Crawford, who gave me the joys of childhood. To my wife, Jackie, who shares with me life's many joys and sorrows. To our children, Eric, Andrea, Joe, and Wes, who have given me joy as a father. And to our grandchildren, Nicolas, Brandon, Katie, Jack, Henry and Hannah, Aria and Ash, who have brought me joy in growing older.

Foreword

by Eric Crawford, Sports Columnist, The Courier-Journal

WHEN I first went to work for The Courier-Journal as a clerk in 1992, it wasn't unusual to have people wander up to me and say, "I've worked here for three years, but I've never met your father."

Indeed, The Courier-Journal building at Sixth and Broadway in Louisville was never a good place to look for Byron Crawford. He never had a desk there. You were better off heading a long way out of town, finding a little general store somewhere off the main road and asking if they'd seen him. Chances are it hadn't been too long since they had.

In 1979, Barry Bingham Jr. installed him as the paper's Kentucky columnist with a great commission—to go therefore into the hills and hollows, the forgotten corners and favorite haunts of his home state, and write about his fellow Kentuckians in his own voice, which was also theirs.

For nearly thirty years, he took his readers into places they lived, or never would have gone. Some days he carried them back in time to a Kentucky as it used to be, or would not continue to be for long. Some mornings, if they were lucky, instead of mountains he would walk them through memories, or his own reflections.

He strived to give his subjects center stage and was reluctant to turn the column toward himself, yet in compilations like this one, now his third collection of pieces from The Courier-Journal to be published, it is hard to miss his unmistakable voice, his sense of a story told right, his feel for expressing the essence of his subjects.

These pieces do tell us something about him. But perhaps they tell me something more. Growing up, I watched him labor over columns on an evolving series of machines, big bulky computers with screens no bigger than today's smart phones, lugging them out to the truck for another run through the state. And I watched him later, when both of us wrote for the same paper, work with the same effort and care. Most of these stories did not shout from the front page of the newspaper, though some did. But he brought front-page dedication to each one.

I know what his work has meant to the state if only because, one-by-one, people tell me now and again about the time he came to interview a family member, and how they still talk about that day, or have framed the column, or read a portion of it at the funeral of someone he wrote about.

He wondered what the interest would be in another collection of columns. I told him if only his friends bought the book, it could take him through two or three printings. Of course, the appeal of his stories is much wider. They've been used in schools and college writing courses, and a while back I even heard of his books being used to teach English to students in Greece.

Truly, you never know where his stories will take you, or where they might wind up. I suppose my best lesson in his eye for a story came a few years ago. He called me to ask about a member of the University of Louisville football marching band whom my mother had seen playing his trumpet from a wheelchair. I told him I didn't know, that I never watched the halftime show.

While I was focused on writing about what I thought was big news, nationally televised football games, I missed something to which he was instinctively drawn. He called several times to ask me if I was sure I didn't want to do that story, but I passed.

Shortly after he wrote his column about blind trumpet player Patrick Henry Hughes and the moving story of his father, who not only pushed him through band practice and performances, but to every class, Sports Illustrated's back page columnist, Rick Reilly, graciously emailed my dad to ask if he could take a crack at writing it, too.

Soon, Hughes was on the national morning shows, and then the Oprah Winfrey Show. His story culminated in the network program Extreme

Home Makeover completely re-doing the Hughes family's house, and millions of Americans were moved by the touching story that was told first in The Courier-Journal by its one writer who saw the value in such stories the most and told them best.

It was an inspiration for many. For me, it was one more example of my dad taking a small story and doing big things.

In the following pages, you'll see what I mean.

Acknowledgments

PRODUCTION of this book would not have been possible without the superb guidance of Courier-Journal archivist Amy Inskeep and the cooperation of the newspaper's management, which granted permission for re-publication of these stories a few years before my retirement in December of 2008.

There are many others to thank, going back to the beginning of my column-writing career in early 1979: Former Courier-Journal publishers Barry Bingham Sr. and Barry Bingham Jr., former executive editor Paul Janensch, and former state editors, friends and mentors, Frank Hartley, James Ausenbaugh, Mark Provano, Gideon Gil, and Deborah Yetter.

I am honored that retired Courier-Journal artist Herman Wiederwohl of Georgetown, Ky., deemed this book worthy of his wonderful illustrations on several pages.

Foremost on the list of those to whom I am indebted are Ray Bertram and Glenn Dean of Stanford, and Melvin Pennington of Danville, who with help from above rescued me from drowning when I was a boy.

Among those to whom special thanks is due for help with stories through the years, or assistance with this book: Hollis Allen and his sister, Alene Slater, of Rocky Ford, Wayne Baxter, Campbellsville, Ron and Carolyn Bland, Bagdad, Dr. James Bland, Lebanon, Bill Bohannon, Elmburg, Joe Bowen, Stanton, Ron Bryant, Georgetown, Margaret Burkett, Paint Lick, Clemens Caldwell, Danville, Lynda Closson, Stanford, David and Shirley Coffman, Liberty, Bonnie Coffee, Shelbyville, Edwin L. Cohen, Louisville, Van Combs Jr., Pleasureville, Ralph Cress, Danville, Keith Cupp, Lexington, Bobby and Geneva Duncan, Strunk, Bill

9

Elam, Frankfort, Cliff and Mary Lloyd Farmer, Shelbyville, Nancy Farmer, Cynthiana, Tim Farmer, Frankfort, Dick and Dorothy Hill Faulkner, Stanford, Thelma Floyd, Bagdad, George Garrison, Stanford, Ted Garrison, Perryville, Buck Goode, Perryville, Walt Gorin, Greensburg, Jodie Hall, Leitchfield, Ray Harm, Sonoita, Arizona, Ray Harm Jr., Pineville, Russ Hatter, Frankfort, Eben Henson, Danville, Joanne Hobbs, Bloomfield, Fred Homra, Fulton.

Howard Howells II, Harrodsburg, Shirley Huff, Munfordville, Jim and Helen Hester, Jeffersontown, Ken and Sue Keller, Pewee Valley, Mark Keller, Falls of Rough, Dennis Kimberling, Moreland, Jeanne Penn Lane, Gravel Switch, Dave Long, Stanford, Chauncey Love, Danville, Porter Maiden, Frakes, Mark Marracinni, Frankfort, Ernie Lee Martin, Jasper Bend, Dr. Larry Martin, Louisville, Thomas McMahan, Campbellsville, Joe and Katherine Miller, Christiansburg, Leo Mudd, Clarkson, John Bearl Murphy, Liberty, Marion Murphy, Liberty, James Riley, Benton, Barbara Rosenman, Ballardsville, Ann Sallee, Springfield, Shirley Sheperson, Danville, Lynda Sherrard, Frankfort, Jim and Donna Sheron, Stanford, Janice Sims, Waynesburg, Harold and Dorothy Slade, Cynthiana, Ken Thompson, Elk Creek, Joan Todd, Louisville, Anthony Trammell, Pine Knot, Dr. William Turner, Lexington, Ed Waggener, Columbia, Sue Wayne, Clinton, Gary West, Bowling Green, Landon Williams, Stanford, Charlie Wilson, Williamstown, Ronnie Young, Corbin.

Special thanks to our intrepid team of folk weather prognosticators, L.H. "Dick" Frymire of Irvington, a "treeologist." Ike Adams of Paint Lick, president of the National Association of Woolly Worm Winter Weather Watchers—(N.A.W.W.W.W.W.), Bill Mardis of Somerset, a counter of fogs in August, and Alene Horner of Jeffersonville, Ind., a persimmon seed splitter, corn shuck and fur reader. Although you were all writers, teachers or business professionals, you were great sports in your chosen fields of weather folklore, and sometimes your winter forecasts beat the real meteorologists!

To the tens of thousands of others who may have written only one note or left a phone message with a story lead for me, I am grateful. In the end, it was your ideas that provided enough material to fill almost three decades of the Kentucky Column with stories from across this great state, some of which fill the pages of this book.

Introduction

THE title of this book, "Kentucky Footnotes," is something of a play on words for all the shoe leather I have worn out, tracking down more than 4,500 stories during nearly three decades as The Courier-Journal's Kentucky Columnist.

While the title should not be taken literally, in an informal sense, the term "footnotes" is most descriptive of much of my work.

The Kentucky Column was often about the fine print of bigger stories; sometimes current, but occasionally from Kentucky history or folklore, or about individuals, places or moments that I thought should not be overlooked.

The column was never designed to grab the headlines, but to bring a distinctively Kentucky flavor to what, through most of my career at the newspaper, was "the Kentucky page," B-1.

When most others were writing about the Kentucky Derby, I was at the horse cemetery on Claiborne Farm near Paris, checking the gravestone of the great Triple Crown winner Secretariat to see who had left flowers.

While many reporters were focusing on a summer cool snap, I was writing about the early 19th Century "Year Without a Summer."

Readers soon realized that I was not chasing the big story, but something different. Ideas began pouring in from across the commonwealth and beyond.

My primary mission with The Courier-Journal, like that of my masterful predecessors Allan Trout and Joe Creason, was to simply tell the stories of Kentucky's people and places – the famous, the exceptional, the ordinary and the infamous – in words and pictures, and to include anything else of interest that I might find along the way.

In the pre-digital era, I was armed with a 35mm Nikon camera, a case of film, pens and notebooks, a tape recorder, portable writing device and a Kentucky map, then was sent on my way to nowhere in particular, but everywhere in general, between the Big Sandy and the Mississippi in the first of many four-wheel-drive vehicles that would cover more than a million miles before I was finished.

This book contains fewer than one year's worth of columns, but they have been selected from three decades during which I wrote for the newspaper. My most difficult task was deciding upon chapter headings. You'll see why when you begin reading through the various subjects that have been squeezed between these covers.

Many of the stories were never printed elsewhere, unless they happened to have been picked up by the Associated Press or another wire service.

On numerous pages I have added my own brand of footnotes containing bits of updated information or brief reflection.

Byron Crawford

PART ONE:

People & Places

Melungeons

November 12, 1995

WISE, Va. – Brent Kennedy is a Melungeon. There is not enough space here to tell the story, even if it were all known. The Melungeons are a mysterious culture whose members have inhabited a few remote settlements in extreme upper east Tennessee, southwest Virginia and southeastern Kentucky since before local history was recorded. They have gradually blended into the general population and are now scattered across the nation.

They typically have dark complexions, but may have blue eyes as well as dark eyes, and often are believed to be of American Indian descent. Kennedy believes there may be 20,000 Kentuckians of some Melungeon ancestry along the Kentucky-Virginia border.

Life in the early days was often difficult for Melungeons, many of whom suffered the same indignities as African Americans, with whom they were frequently accused of sharing a bloodline. Yet there was something distinctly Mediterranean or Middle Eastern about the Melungeons that drew researchers to pry deeper into their past.

Dr. Brent Kennedy, the bright young vice-chancellor of Virginia's Clinch Valley College and author of "The Melungeons—The Resurrection of a Proud People," (Mercer University Press, Macon, Georgia), has emerged as a leading scholar and perhaps the foremost spokesman on the subject.

So compelling are the findings of a thirty member Melungeon Research

Committee which he has assembled, that Turkish television crews are now making visits to families in the mountains along the Kentucky-Virginia border in search of Melungeons. And two of Turkey's most prestigious universities are studying the genetic and historic paths of this nearly forgotten people.

Kennedy owes his quest primarily to a strange disease, erythmea nodosum sarcoidosis, that nearly took his life several years ago. Symptoms mimic those of arthritis, lupus, glaucoma, Hodgkin's and other diseases.

When Kennedy's illness went into remission, he began life anew with a greater appreciation of his family, heritage and time. He learned that sarcoidosis was common among Portuguese immigrants and the Mediterranean peoples. It also was more common in the southeastern United States among both African-Americans and Caucasians of seemingly unrelated backgrounds.

He needed to know how his own Melungeon traits contributed to his illness. Who were these Melungeons who were so much a part of his life but about whom he knew so little?

"Melungeons look different, even within the same family," Kennedy said. "Up Stone Mountain, there's one little boy who looks like he's stepped right out of Istanbul, and his brother who is two years younger looks like he stepped off the boat from Northern Ireland. In one family, you'll see someone who looks Irish, another sibling that looks absolutely Native American, and another that looks Arab, or maybe Turkish, like me. You'd better believe it's caused some problems in some families."

As Kennedy traced his unknown forebears, he found that some had variously

B. CRAWFORD PHOTO OF BRENT KENNEDY FAMILY ARCHIVES OF OLDER PHOTO

claimed to be Portuguese, Indian, Turkish or Moorish. Then he noticed old family names such as Mullins, Collins and Nash that were common in Melungeon lore. A few pieces of the puzzle began falling into place.

For the past five years, Kennedy's research team has traced Melungeons from the dark-complexioned, brown and blue-eyed European-featured people that English and French explorers met in the southern Appalachians during the 1650s to the people who claimed to be "Portyghee" and who the Scotch-Irish settlers found tilling the land when they arrived in the Appalachians late in the next century.

The best historic and scientific evidence indicates that the Spanish colony of Santa Elena was overrun by the English in 1586 at the site of what now is Beaufort, South Carolina, Kennedy says. A band of perhaps 200 survivors fled north and was taken in by the Cherokees near Asheville, North Carolina.

That same year, Sir Francis Drake conquered Cartagena in the southern Caribbean and freed a few hundred Muslim Turks who had been enslaved by the Spanish. A storm forced Drake's fleet toward the North Carolina coast, where he left most of the Turks at Roanoke Island. They soon reached the mainland, mingled with Indians and others who lived along the coast, and eventually moved westward. "So when they claimed to be Portuguese, Turkish, Moorish, Indian and Melungeon, they were telling the truth," said Kennedy, who found that the word "Melungeon" is Turkish, meaning "abandoned by God."

When he visited the Anatolian region of Turkey searching for clues to the lost culture, "they thought I was a Turk," he said, "and I'd look at them and think they could have been from Whitesburg or Virgie, Kentucky. They ate grits, tomato gravy, things that I've eaten in the mountains all my life. The Turkish word, 'gaumy,' which means all messed up, I've heard all my life as 'gaumed up'."

"Probably millions of Americans descended from large numbers of these people who have disappeared into history," Kennedy reflected.

"The evidence is pretty darn strong that Abraham Lincoln's mother, Nancy Hanks, was Melungeon. Elvis Presley's family on his mother's side exited North Carolina at the same time all the other Melungeons did, and headed out West. It's really broad-based ethnic heritage that's sort of been lost in the shuffle of this country's growing."

D-Day DNA

May 25, 2008

A ROMANTIC tragedy of World War II, linked across an ocean by a single strand of DNA, is still unfolding in Kentucky this week. On his deathbed a few years ago, the man Peter Vickery had always believed was his father disclosed that Peter was not his son. Peter's real biological father was an American soldier.

"I felt a bit numb," said Vickery, now 63, a retired truck driver who lives in Birmingham, England.

His 88-year-old mother, who is a patient in a nursing home in England, her mind weakened by a stroke, would later admit to Vickery's younger sisters that, yes, she'd had a brief fling with an American soldier in February 1944 while her husband was serving with British forces in North Africa. She had given birth to Peter, the GI's son, in October 1944. She could no longer remember the soldier's last name – only that his first name was Robert and that he was over six feet tall and in his early 30s. She had never heard from him again after their passionate, fleeting affair in London.

"They had met as part of a foursome, but I don't know with whom, and they had gone out dancing," said Vickery. "I heard that from my sisters. I found it embarrassing to talk with my mother about it."

His mother's heartbroken parents had sent her away from their home in Cardiff to live with an older stepsister in Birmingham after learning that she was pregnant. For a while after her husband returned from the war, she had pretended that Peter was her sister's baby, but the truth finally surfaced.

PHOTO BY BYRON CRAWFORD

Peter Vickery, center, was welcomed to Bardstown by Rick McCubbin, left, and other newly-discovered Kentucky cousins.

Although she and her husband remained married for many years, and even had three other children, they divorced later in life.

"I was kind of glad, really, when I found out that he wasn't my father, because we hadn't gotten along that well most of my life," said Vickery.

In January 2008, Vickery sent a DNA sample to the Web site Ancestry. com, hoping that he might miraculously find some link to his real father.

About the same time, Rick McCubbin, of Bardstown, Ky., an avid genealogist who is the U.S. marshal for the Western District of Kentucky, entered his DNA sample on the same site, hoping to locate McCubbin relatives in Scotland. When notified about their matching DNA a few weeks later, Vickery and McCubbin began exchanging e-mails.

Vickery shared his story with McCubbin and provided his mother's information about a soldier named Robert, over six feet tall and in his 30s, who had passed through England in February 1944.

"Ten minutes later, I get another e-mail back from Rick," said Vickery. "I nearly fell out of my chair."

McCubbin wrote that his great uncle Robert, who was well over six feet, had been in England in early 1944 when he was 32. He had been among the U.S. 29th Infantry Division troops who stormed Omaha Beach on D-Day. He survived the landing but died in battle several weeks later beyond St. Lo. He was never married.

Could Rick McCubbin's great-uncle have been Peter Vickery's father?

Despite the DNA and matching descriptions, McCubbin, who had been a Louisville police officer before he was named U.S. marshal, continued to look for evidence, carefully crosschecking the dates on military records and letters. He sent Vickery the last picture his family had made of Robert Elvis McCubbin, dressed in his Army uniform about 1943, and Vickery showed it to his mother.

"Yes," she was sure the soldier in the picture was Peter's father.

"Her face lit up," Vickery said. "She asked if I would leave the picture with her. She touched my face and said, 'He was a lovely man.'"

Peter Vickery, who is married but has no children, arrived in Kentucky on Tuesday to meet "an extra family" he never knew existed. "I really couldn't afford to come, but when I found out he (Robert) had two sisters alive, I thought I'd better get over here and meet some of these people," he said.

As fate would have it, Rick McCubbin, the family historian, has kept all of his great-uncle's personal effects all these years – the flag from his coffin, his Purple Heart medal, the letters he wrote home, and his wallet containing one dollar and some phone numbers which had been found with his body on the battlefield.

Late last week, McCubbin, Vickery, McCubbin's son, Aaron, Rick's brother, Mike, and their father, Ron, visited the old family graveyard in Hart County and the home on East Kentucky Street in Louisville where Vickery's father lived before the war.

Tomorrow, Rick McCubbin, Vickery and other members of the family will visit the burial site of Robert Elvis McCubbin in Louisville's Evergreen Cemetery where, for the first time in 63 lost Memorial Days, Peter Vickery will finally place a flag on his father's grave.

"That's probably going to get to me," said Vickery. "When your life suddenly changes direction at this time in your life, it's kind of difficult. I've been an Englishman for a long time now, and now I'm newly American."

Footnote: Peter Vickery has since traced the path that his father took after landing at Normandy during the D-Day invasion, and has visited the spot where his father fell a few weeks later. He and his wife are planning more visits with their new family in Bardstown and Louisville and have even discussed moving to Kentucky.

Medal of Honor Overdue

January 1, 2006

THE Army's Military Awards Branch has some unfinished New Year's business regarding one of America's World War II heroes. The late Lt. Garlin Murl Conner of Clinton County, Kentucky, the second most decorated soldier of World War II next to the late Audie Murphy, has been denied the Medal of Honor, despite support for his nomination from seven retired generals, including his own commander, as well as Sen. Robert Dole and numerous Army associations.

The question is why Murphy was awarded the Medal of Honor and Conner was not.

Their repeated acts of valor on the German front were strikingly similar. Both were members of the 3rd Infantry Division, were acquainted with each other and were nearly identical in stature, about five feet-five inches tall, and nearly the same weight.

Conner's citation for the Distinguished Service Cross states that on Jan. 24, 1945, near Houssen, France, he ran 400 yards through an "intense concentration of enemy artillery fire" in the face of six German tanks and tank destroyers and 600 German soldiers, "assaulting in full fury the spearhead position held by his battalion."

Disregarding enemy fire, Conner, who had slipped away from a military hospital with a serious hip wound to rejoin his unit rather than return home to Kentucky, unreeled a telephone wire, plunged into a shallow ditch in front of the battle line and "calmly directed round after round of

23

artillery for three hours as enemy troops surged forward in waves, sometimes to within five yards of his position."

As the Germans mounted an all-out assault, Conner, armed with a Thompson submachine gun, ordered American artillery to concentrate on his own position, "resolved to die if necessary to halt the enemy."

He is credited with killing about 50 German soldiers and wounding an estimated 150 in the engagement while saving many American soldiers.

Murphy's Medal of Honor citation states that when six tanks and waves of German infantry attacked his company on January 26, near Holtzwhir, France, he ordered his men to withdraw while he remained and gave artillery fire directions by telephone. With the enemy on three sides, Murphy climbed onto a burning tank destroyer and turned its .50-caliber machine gun against the Germans, holding the position for an hour and receiving a wound in the leg as Germans closed to within ten yards.

After running out of ammunition, Murphy made his way back to his company, refused medical attention, and directed a counterattack. He was credited with killing or wounding about 50 of the enemy.

Both soldiers were involved in numerous other battlefield heroics and received many citations for bravery. Conner, wounded seven times, was awarded four Silver Stars; Murphy was wounded three times and was awarded three Silver Stars. Conner was wounded in the landing at Anzio, but Murphy was hospitalized with an illness and did not make the invasion.

"The Army Decorations Board determined that the degree of action and service rendered (by Conner) did not meet the strict criteria for the proposed award," Lt. Col. William H. Johnson, chief of the Military Awards Branch, wrote to Walton Haddix of the Clinton County Historical Society in early December.

"If his citation is equal to Audie Murphy's, the most decorated hero of all wars, how can you say he doesn't deserve this medal?" asked Haddix, a former naval officer.

The effort to have the Medal of Honor awarded to Conner began nearly ten years ago when retired Green Beret Richard Chilton of Wisconsin discovered Conner's records of heroism while researching the war records of an uncle whom Conner had risked his life to save at Anzio.

Due largely to the efforts of Chilton and Haddix, many have endorsed

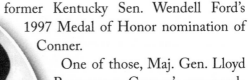

former Kentucky Sen. Wendell Ford's 1997 Medal of Honor nomination of Conner.

One of those, Maj. Gen. Lloyd Ramsey, was Conner's commander and knew both Conner and Murphy. He has said that while Murphy was "an outstanding soldier in every way," Conner was "the finest soldier I've ever seen" and deserves the Medal of Honor "more than any man I've ever heard of."

The burden of wartime duties and Conner's modesty were factors in his not having been nominated at the time of his acts of heroism, the general said.

Garlin M. Conner, 1st Lt. 1945, "K" Company, 3rd Battalion, 7th Regiment, 3rd Division

Conner died in 1998 in Clinton County, where he served seventeen years as president of the Clinton County Farm Bureau. During his free time, he traveled much of Kentucky, assisting veterans with paperwork regarding benefits.

General Ramsey has requested to appear before an Army board to make an appeal for the Medal of Honor for Conner, but so far has been denied.

Now, Chilton said, he and many others who have taken up the cause can only hope that someone in the complex chain of command will see fit to present Conner's widow, Pauline, and his family with the posthumous award for Conner's valor, or at least offer a reasonable explanation for its refusal. Lt. Conner deserves that much.

Footnote: If the Medal of Honor is ever awarded to Conner, he will become the most decorated soldier of World War II.

Nagasaki A-Bomb Survivor

August 13, 1995

FIFTY years ago last Wednesday, 14-year-old Aiko Nakashima was hurrying along a busy street in Nagasaki, Japan, when she heard the distant drone of a large airplane high above the broken clouds. She had grown accustomed to air raids in the port city, but she heard no air-raid sirens that morning.

"I stopped and looked up. I didn't see anything. So I said, 'Well, maybe I was imagining things,'" she remembers. "I looked at other people, and evidently, they had not heard, because they were just walking. So I start to walk again, then I heard it again. But that time a little bit closer. Then I looked up, and I still didn't see any plane, but I saw a parachute coming down with some shiny object." Seconds later the atomic bomb detonated barely a mile away.

"The next thing, there was a big flash – boom! Like that. I throw myself on the ground … and when I hit the ground, at the same time, there was a blast wave or heat ray, so hot, just a tremendous wind blew through," she said.

"A horrible roaring noise. I can't get it off my mind even now. There is no other sound like that. Not even a tornado. A tornado would sound like a baby chime compared to that big roar. Everything turned black."

Many years later, Aiko would learn that the shiny object she had seen descending by parachute was a sonde, a probe used to record the shock waves of the bomb that would devastate Nagasaki a moment later, killing an estimated 75,000 people.

By some almost miraculous twist of circumstance, Aiko was not killed. She worked with other schoolgirls every day at the giant Mitsubishi torpedo plant – the bomb target. But at her mother's insistence, she had stayed home that morning to see a doctor about a fever she was running from a throat infection. Then she had tried to catch three streetcars to go to the plant, but they had all been full, so she had begun walking toward the factory just before 11 a.m. Her watch stopped at 11:03.

No one at the torpedo factory or on the streetcars survived.

Aiko lay motionless in the darkness, her fingers covering her eyes, her thumbs over her ear canals, her mouth open to equalize air pressure – as Japanese schoolchildren had been taught to do when bombs fell.

She barely parted her fingers and peeped out into the eerie, silent darkness that soon awakened with fires and cries of death and suffering. An air-raid siren wailed. Her mouth was full of dirt. She heard someone say, "This must be the end of the world."

As light began to return, she joined a pitiful mob of mangled people, trying to run from the intense heat that enveloped them.

"Some of them were burned from head to toe. Some, their hair was gone, and clothes burned and gone. And of course the back of my clothes was completely gone," Aiko said. "And everybody's eyes bulged out, the same expression – not looking any place. Everybody said, 'Hot, hot, hot.'"

"… In the meantime, here a B-29 came, very low, so I ran to the bomb shelter. … The smell of burning human flesh was awful."

Many of Aiko's schoolmates and teachers died in the bombing, but her family survived. Aiko eventually recovered from severe burns and radiation sickness, and graduated from the university with a degree in English.

By 1953, she was working as an interpreter at a U.S. Air Force base off the coast of Japan. There she met, fell in love with, and married Air Force Lt. Don Allen of Henderson, Ky.

Although their parents bitterly opposed the marriage, Aiko came to Henderson County that same year to take her place beside her husband on the family's large farm. Their families later accepted the marriage. The Allens have raised six children, none of whom have so far suffered any known effects of radiation, although Aiko has been troubled with poor health most of her life.

She has returned to Nagasaki several times, but she cannot bring herself to visit the museum that commemorates the bombing. Now, a half-century and half a world away from Nagasaki, she is philosophical about what happened that morning when she was 14.

"If it wasn't a bomb, we would have been killed anyway," she said. "We were taught to fight till the last. Why bring it up? It's done. You can never bring it back. It's no use to keep pressing it."

Aiko Allen was only a mile from the Nagasaki atomic bomb target.

PHOTO BY BYRON CRAWFORD

Footnote: Aiko Allen died in her sleep about eight years after this story was written.

Meteorite Man

January 4, 1988

CRESTWOOD, Ky. – How many times have you seen a meteor plummeting to Earth and wondered if you could find it?
The chances are slim, but it does happen, says geologist Charlie Oldham, whose collection of more than 10,000 rocks contains one rare piece of a meteorite.

"I was walking on a farm here in Oldham County, on the banks of the Ohio River upstream from Eighteen Mile Island more than 10 years ago, when I found it," Oldham said. "Anything that looks unusual, I usually poke at or kick at. I was carrying a walking stick at the time I hit that thing, and it didn't budge. It just went 'clunk.' And anything that has a metallic sound, I usually pick up."

The chunk of meteorite, just smaller than the palm of his hand, weighs between one-quarter and one-half pound and is composed mostly of nickel and iron.

Some meteorites, commonly referred to as "shooting stars," burn up before they reach Earth's surface. Others miss the Earth completely. Those that reach Earth often exploded into several pieces before striking the ground.

"They're called meteors until they're on the ground. Then they are meteorites," Oldham explained. "There are estimates that hundreds of thousands of tons of material, from microscopic size to larger, hit the Earth every year. Of course, a lot of them end up in the oceans.

"I'd say there are probably 10 findable pieces, large enough to see, that

29

hit an area the size of Kentucky every year. But not all are metallic. A lot are what are called 'stony,' that are alien to this environment, and they break down rather rapidly into unrecognizable lumps."

Most of the meteorites have been found by farmers, not scientists, Oldham noted. Many of those discovered in Kentucky and other agricultural states were found during the years when farmers used horses and small tractors.

"Now that they've started getting these very large machines, they're so far removed from the ground that they don't see arrowheads or anything," Oldham said.

Geological records indicate meteorites that may have weighed several pounds each fell in Whitley County near Cumberland Falls and near Walltown in Casey County in 1919.

In February 1977, when he was a graduate student at the University of Louisville, Oldham helped investigate a meteorite that crashed through the porch of a house in Louisville.

PHOTO COURTESY OF ARCHIVES

Oldham holds a meteorite fragment found near the Ohio River in Oldham County.

"I'm not real good with astrophysics...but essentially, the thing came slicing through the atmosphere and blew up somewhere over the city of Louisville," Oldham said.

"Fragments of it fell in a number of places. I think they found some pieces down on Market Street in the gutter, and the big piece–approximately fist size–went through this man's roof and buried itself in the ground beneath his porch."

Courier-Journal records indicate that the meteorite crashed through the porch of a West End home at 4509 Greenwood Avenue, which then was the residence of Robert Barlow.

Not many people experience such close encounters with meteorites, but Oldham said there are records of meteorite fragments striking a few humans. He recalls one account of a meteorite having penetrated the engine block of a moving car.

Since meteors are seen mostly at night, and only then for a dazzling second or two, Oldham said it is virtually impossible to judge how far away they might be.

"You can see something that you'll think has landed a mile away, and it may be 40 or more," he said. "But if you hear a sound (some have heard a crackling noise from meteors at close range), you are within about 1,000 feet of one, I'd say, the size of your fist. And if you see an intense blue light, like an electrical discharge, or smell a sulfurous or acid odor, I'd say you are between 300 and 500 feet away from it."

Oldham, who works for the Kentucky Department of Surface Mining when he is not rock collecting, gets about 150 inquiries a year from people who want him to examine strange rocks they have found–suspected meteorites, fossils, unidentified minerals and Indian relics.

"If somebody says it came out of the sky, I'll be there as soon as I can get there," he said. "If it's been found in a field or somewhere, I'll try and get there within a week...If I don't get out and look at it, it'll bug me forever."

Another Old
Kentucky Home

March 14, 2004

THERE were moments in Liberia, as Ernie Martin peered
through the viewfinder of his video camera, when the Kentucky
in Africa seemed as close to the Kentucky of his birth as a hug,
a handshake or a song.

"When we met Mary Dixon and she broke into her version of 'My
Old Kentucky Home,' that was the moment of connection," said Martin, a Kentucky Educational Television producer and videographer. "They
treated us like it was a family homecoming."

Martin had been hoping for such a moment for several years, as
he combed over bits of history about a colony called Kentucky, Liberia, which was founded in the early 1830s by former slaves from the
commonwealth.

The forty square-mile area that once was known as Kentucky is now
generally known by the name of its former capital and largest town,
Clay-Ashland, which took its name from a founder of the American
Colonization Society, statesman Henry Clay, and his Lexington estate,
Ashland.

"What impressed me most about it was the hills," Martin said. "Every
place else was real flat, until I got to Kentucky. Coming up the St. Paul
River from Monrovia on a boat, it looked like the kind of place you'd want

to stop and stay if you were from Kentucky. It was a beautiful spot."

As Martin approached Clay-Ashland, 170 years after the first of more than 600 colonists arrived from the United States, he at first saw more churches than houses. Most of the outlying houses in the area of about 20,000 people were mud and bamboo huts and structures ravaged by more than twenty years of civil war. But to Martin's surprise, in the main town of Clay-Ashland, there were a number of once grand dwellings reminiscent of Kentucky architecture.

Everywhere there were friendly people who greeted him and his trip coordinator, attorney Mark Paxton of Lexington.

"They had no idea we were coming," Martin said. "The first words I said were, 'Greetings from Kentucky in America!' About twelve people gathered around, and they just kept coming."

Mary Dixon, a deaconess at the First Baptist Church of Clay-Ashland, knew the story of Kentucky, Liberia, and understood why Martin had come.

"We have been praying for this day, that one day we would be able to see somebody, someone would come from Kentucky," Dixon said on camera. "We want them to know that we still live in the city of Kentucky. Our history is a great history that we can never forget, about Kentucky."

As a child, Dixon, who is in her 40s, could remember a community "induction program" in which she heard a woman singing, "Take me back to my old Kentucky home."

"She was dressed like she was coming from Kentucky," Dixon told Martin.

"She had on this long dress, puffed sleeves, and she had her hair fixed in that style, and she told us that's how the immigrants came and they were dressed."

Baptist church pastor Jeremiah Walker, who is much older, could remember hearing local bands playing Stephen Foster's version of "My Old Kentucky Home." During a

PHOTO BY BYRON CRAWFORD

Ernie Martin

33

Youngsters in front of a church and school in Clay-Ashland

dinner and singing in honor of Martin's visit, the townspeople shared their stories and memories about Kentucky, Liberia.

"The story has been told over and over and over through many generations, but it's pretty much a legend and they know very little about this Kentucky," Martin said.

At least two of Liberia's presidents were descendants of colonists from Kentucky. One of Martin's hosts was Benoni Urey, who said he has ancestral connections to colonists from Princeton, Kentucky, and who owns a cell-phone company and a large farming operation in Liberia.

In Monrovia, Liberia's capital, Martin found Kentucky Fried Chicken on a restaurant menu. Not KFC, but the restaurant's own recipe. He found roads with familiar names and a river named "Farmington," and he heard of a little town called "Lexington."

There once were keepsakes in the region that could be traced to the early settlers from Kentucky, Martin was told. But the only one that he found to have survived the looting of the civil war was a cast iron farm implement that had been brought from the commonwealth by the family of former Liberian President William David Coleman, who came from

Lexington. The unidentified tool, made in Seneca, New York, is now used for cracking palm nuts and is stored at a police station.

Local residents told Martin that a man named George Washington, who had grown up in Clay-Ashland, had immigrated to Kentucky a few years ago and had written to say, "I'm back in my old home, Kentucky in America." Martin said he hopes to locate Washington, if he still lives in Kentucky.

"I promised that I would send them pictures and documents that they may have never had or may have lost because of the war," Martin said.

"Oh, I would like to send (Kentuckians) greetings," Mary Dixon told Martin during an interview, "and tell them we are proud to see our brothers come back to find out about us. I will be happy if, as things get better, we will have an exchange relationship. I wish that, when I get there, I get to Kentucky and be able to meet with my people."

Locomotive Whistle-Players

June 15, 1987

DANVILLE, Ky. – It's been years since the hills of south central Kentucky resounded to the hymn "Oh, How I Love Jesus," played by Charles "Dutch" Eiford on the whistle of a steam locomotive. But there are still a few who haven't forgotten what beautiful music it was.

"He'd start playing it when he came out of the tunnel, going south onto the Cumberland River bridge, and whatever our family was doing, we'd stop and listen until he got through," recalled Bernice Mitchell, 84, of Burnside in Pulaski County. "When he got about to Tateville, he gave a little long toot. I don't know whether it was an 'amen' or not."

Chauncey Love of Danville, 70, a retired Southern Railway conductor, remembers Eiford as "a jolly, Santa Claus type fellow."

"I had a dancing doll that you'd put on a board and peck the board, and that doll would dance up a storm," Love said. "Dutch took up with that doll, and he took it and carried it all over town, and I think his daughter might have made some clothes for it."

Several Southern Railway steam locomotive engineers are said to have played songs on the train whistles, including one named McGraw who preached on the side, and another named McMurray, both of whom are said to have been proficient.

PHOTO COURTESY OF C.L. LOVE

"Dutch" Eiford, far left, in the Danville yards, early '40s

"McGraw was a little bit before my time," said retired fireman Bill Rowbottom, 73, of Moreland, Kentucky. "I started to work in 1937; McMurray died in about 1938 or 1939."

Eiford, who was born in Greenup County in 1887 and died in Danville in 1961, once told a writer of railroad stories that he learned to play the whistle on lonesome runs through the Cumberland Mountains while working for the old Louisville & Nashville Railroad. That was prior to his years with the former CNO & TP (Cincinnati, New Orleans and Texas Pacific), now Southern Railway.

By the 1930s and 1940s, folks along the Southern tracks had come to look forward to serenades from the whistle-playing engineers whose magnificent steam engines churned through the valleys and around the mountains near their homes.

There is a widely told story that a preacher who was holding a tent meeting near the depot at Stearns, in McCreary County, paused during his sermon to permit his congregation to listen as Eiford played "Oh How I Love Jesus" when the locomotive rumbled through town. As the strains of the hymn died out, the preacher is said to have remarked in a trembling voice that only a religious man could whistle the hymn as that engineer had done.

The next night, however, on the train's return trip, the preacher and congregation were stunned to hear Eiford playing "How Dry I Am."

Soon afterward, the story goes, the division superintendent sent Eiford a letter advising him to use steam for pulling cars instead of for entertaining the citizens of Stearns.

Although some of the whistles were adjusted for tone, there apparently was no substitute for practice and a good ear for music among the rugged men who learned to play them.

"When I was a child, Dutch would come through Stearns about 11 o'clock at night, and my grandmother would wake me up to hear him play the hymn on the whistle," said Lucille Horn, 70, of Danville, whose late husband, E.S. Horn, was a retired Southern Railway engineer.

As far as anyone knows, "Oh, How I Love Jesus" and "How Dry I Am" were the only two songs that Eiford ever mastered on the whistle, although it is reported that Bully King, another hymn whistling engineer, could play "Nearer My God to Thee."

When the last of the steam locomotives disappeared in the early 1950s, the whistle playing engineers were silenced, eventually retired, and faded into obscurity.

But there are still a few folks in the small communities within earshot of the Southern Railway tracks who remember the thrill of hearing "Oh How I Love Jesus" echoing through the hills on a moonlit night, when Dutch Eiford had a full head of steam and was in the mood to play.

Enemies But Friends

September 3, 1990

A NTIOCH, Ky. — His simple marble headstone is leaning
slightly southward, seemingly anchored to the North only by a
faded little American flag left by an unknown visitor to Pendleton County's Richland Baptist Church Cemetery.

The weathered inscription on the gravestone reads, "Wagoner Thos.
Bradford, Co. B., 40th Ky. Inf." It is about all that is left of Bradford's story, except in the memory of his grandson, 89-year-old Hollis Bradford, a
retired Fleming County farmer who was told the story by his father, who
heard it from his father, the Civil War veteran himself.

Hollis Bradford can recall having seen his grandfather only once when
he was three and the crippled old man with a long white beard came to
their house in Fleming County.

But when Hollis Bradford was older, working beside his father in the
fields, he came to know the high price his grandfather had paid to fight
for the Union, and of a wartime friendship that transcended even his
grandfather's fierce loyalty to the Union cause.

Before Wagoner Thomas Bradford enlisted in Co. B. 40th Ky. Mounted Infantry in June 1863 at Falmouth, his father told him that if he sided
with the North in the war, he would be disinherited, and he was.

Nonetheless, the young Bradford rode off on the Union side.

Years later, he told his son, Hollis Bradford's father, that some of his
term of service was spent guarding a bridge in central Kentucky in the

vicinity of Mercer and Boyle counties where, for a time, the Confederate army had a guard posted at one end of the bridge and the Union had a guard at the other end.

Bradford eventually became friends with a Confederate soldier from Alabama who guarded the far end of the bridge.

"They tried to holler across the river at one another, and finally one day one of them said, 'Stick your bayonet in the ground and come out on the bridge, and let's get close enough so we can talk'," Hollis Bradford said.

"They decided they'd draw a line on the bridge and each one would stay on his side of the line. They met almost every day, and played checkers and talked about their families. They traded tobacco and, if one caught more fish than the other, they divided them. They were perfect friends on everything but war, and each one was dedicated to the cause for which he was fighting."

Historian Rebecca Conover of Mercer County is unsure which bridge might have been the subject of Bradford's story, but she says that journals of the Shakers who had a settlement in Mercer County near the Kentucky River indicate that both Union and Confederate forces did sometimes share the crossings along the river in that area.

Several years after the war, Hollis Bradford's father said that he witnessed a strange re-union while working in the field with his father.

"My dad said they saw a man coming, riding a mule, and that my grandfather went to meet him," Hollis Bradford said. "The man got off his mule, and they shook hands and talked a minute, and the fellow pulled something out of his pocket and showed it to grandfather, and he looked at it and handed it back, and they talked a while longer and the man got on the mule and left."

Later, when Hollis Bradford's father asked who the stranger was, his father told him that one day during the war, while guarding the bridge, he got orders to dispose of the Confederate guard on the other side before Union troops crossed the bridge the next day.

"My dad said my grandfather told him, "Well, son, I guess I can tell you what happened. I overpowered him and threw his gun in the river, and told him that if he ever wanted to see his family, to get lost in the bushes.' He said, "That man rode from Alabama, across Tennessee and half way across Kentucky to say, Thank you."

The story is one of thousands about the War Between the States that has been virtually lost to history, surviving only by word of mouth from one generation to the next. Hollis Bradford said he doesn't remember ever hearing the name of the Confederate soldier whose life his grandfather spared.

But perhaps somewhere in Alabama, a nearly forgotten story has been passed down through the descendants of a Confederate soldier who told of his unique friendship with a Union soldier on a bridge somewhere in Kentucky.

And maybe, in a lonesome cemetery in Alabama, there is a weathered gravestone that leans slightly northward, bearing the name of a Confederate veteran who once rode a mule all the way to Kentucky just to say, "Thank you."

Her Father's Story

December 17, 2006

MUNFORDVILLE, Ky. - Her father had no name until he
was grown. He was born into slavery, taken from his parents
as an infant, and brought up on a large plantation somewhere
in Southern Kentucky, said his youngest daughter, Bertha Mae Rogers,
82, of Munfordville.

She remembers listening to his stories, when he was very old and she
was a child; of his being given the task of carrying water to other slaves
in the field when he was a youngster, and of being whipped by overseers
if he spilled water. Each time slaves were herded to the auction block, he
had hoped that someone who would not mistreat him might buy him, he
told her. "But nobody would buy him because he was too small," Rogers
said. "He was always a small man, but he could work."

When her father reached the approximate age of 20, he ran away from
the plantation one night and finally wound up knocking on the door of
another plantation house, possibly near Metcalfe County.

Trembling with fear and hunger, he asked for something to eat.

The owner of the plantation, a man named Bradley, fed him, and gave
him lodging for the night. The next morning, when slave-catchers with
tracking hounds showed up at the door, Bradley bought Rogers' father,
and gave him the name Abner Bradley. The new owner treated him with
kindness, her father recalled. He was taught to read, write and count,
and was allowed to sing, laugh and have conversations with other slaves

without being punished.
"Until he was given a
name (in 1855), he was
not recognized as a per-
son," Rogers said. "This
brought tears to Papa's
eyes. He that was nobody
had become somebody."

Rogers' 1989 story
about her father in the
Hart County Historical
Society Quarterly led to
the publication in 2004
of "Wounded But Not
Broken," a collection of
the stories he had hand-
ed down. She has since
written a sequel, "The
Enduring Legacy."

In the two self-pub-
lished narratives, edited
by her daughter Vickie

Bertha Mae Rogers

PHOTO BY BYRON CRAWFORD

Rogers Armstrong of Columbus, Ga., she describes how her father was
freed, became a sharecropper, married and had children, then lost his
first wife to an illness and later, when he was well up in years, remarried a
young woman and had another family.

The last walk she remembered taking with her father was to a local
store after he had seen her trying to place cardboard over the holes in
her shoe soles during the later years of the Great Depression. She saw
tears cloud his eyes when a storekeeper turned them away after her
father asked for credit to buy her a pair of slippers. The storekeeper was
afraid that, due to her father's advanced age, he could die before the bill
was paid.

"All he had on for a belt was a string tied around his waist," she said.
"He was walking with a cane and holding my hand."

She and her father then walked two miles to a secondhand-clothing
store where the owner, whom her father had once cared for as a child,

welcomed them and gave her three pairs of shoes, "two pairs for school and one pair for church."

After they returned home, Rogers said her father got into bed and never got up again. He died five days later, in April 1935, possibly beyond the age of 100. She was 11. Her mother never remarried. Bertha Mae Rogers would grow up to graduate from Simmons Bible College, and would serve as a district missionary and teacher of adult literacy classes in Hart County. She is the grandmother of Kentucky's 1992 "Mr. Basketball" and later University of Louisville starting guard "Tick" Rogers.

In her 80th year, she would write her father's stories for other generations to remember long after she is gone. "The young man that had given me slippers gave Mama a suit for Papa to be buried in," she said. "I have never been able to find Papa's gravestone."

Civil War Daughter

September 25, 2005

BETHELRIDGE, Ky. – If she is not the last Kentucky daughter of a Union Civil War soldier, Eva Watson Martin is unquestionably among the few. Martin, 91, a resident of Bethelridge in rural Casey County, is the youngest of 14 children of John Green Watson, a member of the 1st Kentucky Union Cavalry, Company A.

"He was married three times, and I was the only child from his last marriage," Martin said. "His first wife was my mom's aunt, and I was raised up close to their granddaughters. One of the girls asked me one day, 'Can you figure out what relation we are?' I said, 'Lord, no.'"

Martin has a photograph that she believes was made in 1916 of herself and one of her father's great–granddaughters – both about age two – sitting on the old soldier's knees.

Watson married Martin's mother, Quintilla Carman, in November 1908, when he was 73 and Carman was 36.

"My mom told me one time that somebody asked her, 'What did you want with that old man?'" Martin recalled. "She said, 'I wanted him because I loved him'."

Martin was born in the summer of 1914, when her father turned 79. His oldest child, a daughter from his first marriage, was already 54 when Martin arrived, but the two became close friends.

"Real daughters and real sons are quite rare ... and they're always treated like celebrities if we can get them to come to the National

45

Encampment," said John A. Mills of Lexington, an offi- cer with the Sons of Union Veterans of Kentucky. "The scenario is, the father was in his 70s or 80s, and was in his second or third marriage – to a young woman."

Mills is aware of no more than three or four children of Union soldiers still living in Kentucky. One of them, Charlie Brock of London, is a member of Lexington's Elijah P. Marrs camp of the Sons of Union Veterans of the Civil War.

Eva Watson Martin, 91, holds this photograph of her father, John Green Watson, taken in 1916. Eva is sitting in his lap along with his great-granddaughter Estella Ware, when both girls were about two years old.

Martin doesn't remember any of her now–deceased old- er half brothers and half sisters talking much about their fa- ther's Civil War service, but a few stories were passed down through the family. They in- clude her father's story about going to sleep one winter night beside a log – with the reins of his horse's bridle tied around his wrist – and waking the next morning covered with snow.

Both Watson and his father, who later attained the rank of captain in another unit, rode with Col. Frank Lane Wolford's cavalry. The 1st Ken- tucky saw action in the battles of Perryville, Wildcat Mountain and Mill Springs, and spent much of the war in pursuit of Confederate Gen. John Hunt Morgan.

Watson died in 1920 at age 85.

"I lacked a little bit, being six years old when he died, and wouldn't have remembered it even if he'd told me a lot of stuff," Martin said. "But I remember that he was always trading horses. And I can remember that he got a new one that jumped up on the wooden gate and broke it down, and that I went to the house and got under the bed and cried."

She remembers seeing her father sick in bed and remembers his death. He is buried in the Valley Oak Baptist Church Cemetery just down the road from her farm, at the church where she is the oldest member.

Somewhere, she has a Civil War medal that had belonged to her father, but she wasn't able to find it.

Perhaps the most important keepsake that John Green Watson provided his youngest daughter was the 90-acre farmstead where she and her late husband, Ralph, made their living and raised a family of two sons and a daughter.

"I drew a pension from his Civil War service till I was 21," Martin said. "My mom never did spend it, she saved it for me. That's what I bought this farm with."

Footnote: Eva Watson Martin died in the summer of 2009.

Six Months to Live

May 28, 2003

BRIDGEPORT, Ky. – This is a story for everyone who has been given only six months to live. "I know how they feel," said 97-year-old Hubert Craig of Franklin County. "That's what doctors told me almost 55 years ago, but I'm still here."

Craig, then 44 and head cashier of the Detroit office of a large insurance company, suffered a heart attack on his way to work in May 1947.

He was treated by doctors at Detroit's Ford Hospital and underwent months of tests and examinations, all of which yielded grim results.

"The two heart doctors that I had were, at that time, leading cardiologists of the country, and one was my very good friend," Craig said. "In the fall of 1948 they just said, 'We can't do any more for you. If you're real careful, you might make it six months.'"

Both doctors are, of course, long since deceased, while Craig still lives on the farm he bought in Central Kentucky, where he had planned to "die peacefully" well over half a century ago.

He was born in Indianapolis and had worked in Lexington before transferring to Detroit. Both he and his late wife, Lena, a lawyer, loved the Bluegrass. After Hubert's terminal prognosis, he resigned his job and the couple moved back to Kentucky, bought a historic farm home several miles west of Frankfort and began renovating the house. Hubert, still alive and growing stronger after six months, decided to become a cattle farmer.

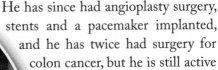

He has since had angioplasty surgery, stents and a pacemaker implanted, and he has twice had surgery for colon cancer, but he is still active for a man who was born in February 1906.

"I've been sick a lot, but I ran 200 head of cattle every year and cut all this hay and helped load it," he said. "And I worked thirteen years part-time as a cashier at Keeneland Race Course and twelve years at Churchill Downs."

His sister, Clara Saffell, 82, who now shares the home with her brother, describes Craig as having "a lot of grit" and determination.

He does take several medications. "I think the good Lord and medicine have kept him going," Saffell said. "But at least he's still going."

"If I live to be 100, I'll never forget how it felt when they sat me down and told me face-to-face that I just had six months to live. Your priorities change in a hurry," Craig said.

"Sometimes when I hear of somebody being given only a few months to live, I think, 'If I could just see that person, I'd tell them I'm a living example that the doctors can be wrong.'"

Footnote: Hubert Craig died in April 2007, at the age of 101.

Gift of Life

September 23, 2007

WHAT if one of your best friends desperately needed a kidney transplant and you were the most promising donor cross-match?

Amy Covert told her friend Kerri Cope, "I'm going to do it."

"Amy literally saved my life," Cope said last week while recuperating from the transplant at her Frankfort home. "It's no different than if somebody were to push a baby stroller out of the way of an oncoming car."

Covert, 35, and Cope, 34, both state employees, have been close friends for several years. Covert, who is single and also lives in Frankfort, introduced Cope to a former co-worker, Bryce Fields, whom Cope would later marry. Both the bride and groom were so fond of Covert that they insisted she perform the ceremony.

"Amy was ordained a minister (and bonded) just so she could marry us," said Bryce Fields.

Early this year, when Cope learned that she would need her second kidney transplant in 15 years, several family members, and friends volunteered for tests to find a potential donor. But Covert emerged as the best candidate.

"I felt very fortunate that I'm healthy enough to be able to do this," said Covert. "Maybe the reason I didn't think that long and hard about it goes back to sort of the way I was raised. All my life I watched both

50

Amy Covert and Kerri Cope

my mother and my father give to other people."

The first words of her mother, Sue Covert, upon learning of the decision were, "I can see you doing that, Amy."

After months of testing and consultation, the combined five-hour surgeries took place at the University of Kentucky Medical Center on Aug. 15.

"I held it together pretty well until we were side by side just before the surgery and I just lost it," Cope said. "I started crying as soon as I saw her, and said, 'I'll never be able to repay you for this. All I can do is just take this gift and live my life as best I can.'"

Separate surgical teams removed and implanted Covert's left kidney into Cope, describing the surgery as having gone perfectly.

"The kidney was working so well right after the transplant that they had to give me potassium, magnesium and sodium supplements, because it was filtering out so much that it was taking some of my nutrients with it," said Cope. "It's immediate. You wake up and just suddenly have energy. I wanted to get up and walk."

Now, Covert and Cope have turned their attention to helping other Kentucky state government employees who may be organ or bone marrow donors get necessary sick leave.

They have sent a proposal to state Sen. Julian Carroll for "Gift of Life" legislation that would give a state employee five days of sick leave for bone marrow donations and 30 days to recover from a major organ donation.

"Seventeen states already have such legislation," said Cope. "And some also offer tax deductions for reimbursement of expenses for people who might not have the ability to take off work."

The Four Chaplains

January 28, 2007

D ON ROTH never lets me forget the four chaplains.
Each year at this time, when many others are preoccupied with the Super Bowl and basketball, Oscar nominations, politics and foreign conflicts, Roth, a retired Louisville jeweler and bookstore owner, leaves a simple message on my work phone that the anniversary of the four chaplains is coming up on February 3rd.

One year he had just arrived home from a thirteen-week hospital stay when he called to remind me, "We must never forget."

The 82-year-old Army Air Force veteran never knew the four chaplains, but he has accumulated a two-inch-thick clipping file about their selfless acts of heroism aboard the sinking U.S. troop ship Dorchester in 1943.

The four chaplains, all first lieutenants, were George L. Fox, a Methodist pastor from Vermont; Alexander D. Goode, a rabbi from Pennsylvania; Clark V. Poling of the Dutch Reform Church in America, New York state; and John P. Washington, a Catholic priest from New Jersey.

Three were in their early 30s. Fox, the 42-year-old father of two, had enlisted in the Army on the same day his 18-year-old son joined the Marines. Poling had one infant son and another child on the way. Goode had a young daughter.

The Dorchester departed New York on January 23rd with more than 900 new soldiers. The ship was torpedoed by Germans off Greenland just after midnight on February 3rd, and sank 27 minutes later.

As the vessel was being swallowed up by the icy North Atlantic, eyewitnesses told of seeing the chaplains passing out life jackets and comforting frightened young soldiers.

When the life jacket boxes were empty, each chaplain removed his own life jacket and gave it to a soldier who had none. Then they helped calm the fears of many terrified soldiers who were afraid to jump overboard, their only hope of being saved.

The war department reported many months after the tragedy that 230 soldiers were rescued, but that nearly 700 others, including the four chaplains, had gone down with the ship in the darkness.

As the Dorchester was sinking, survivors told of seeing the four chaplains, arms locked together and bracing themselves against the deck railing, praying and singing hymns until they disappeared into the water.

One survivor remembered the moment as "the finest thing I have ever seen this side of heaven."

ILLUSTRATION BY WEIDERWOHL

Kentuckian Glenn Porter of Ohio County, an 8th Army Air Force veteran of World War II who narrowly missed being one of the troops aboard the Dorchester, remembered hearing at the time of the tragedy that "it was easier for those four chaplains of different faiths to die together than it is for the rest of us of different faiths to live together."

The chaplains were posthumously awarded Purple Hearts, Distinguished Service Crosses, and a special congressional Four Chaplains Medal for valor. A stained glass window in Washington's National Cathedral commemorates their sacrifice.

I've seen artist's drawings of what they think the scene might have looked like with the Four Chaplains onboard ship," said Roth. "I can't imagine four men agreeing to give up their life jackets and sink and drown in the middle of the ocean, so that four other people anonymous to them could survive."

Roth has never been able to find words to express his admiration for the chaplains' compassion and courage. But again this year, as in many years past, he quietly did what he could.

He called to ask that I remind anyone who might read this that February 3rd will be the anniversary of the deaths of the four chaplains, and that no one should ever forget their sacrifice, or the lessons for living that they left us in dying.

Nonesuch, Monkey's Eyebrow, Rabbit Hash and Other Great Places

November 6, 1996

ONESUCH, Ky. — It is a fine name, "Nonesuch." One that ought to be preserved as long as the Woodford County settlement survives, and even beyond.

Yet, if you drive to Nonesuch to visit the large Irish Acres antiques gallery and gourmet restaurant that now occupy the former Nonesuch Elementary School, or to have a sandwich in the country store there, or to just enjoy the rambling hillsides lined with stone fences, you probably will never see a sign that says "Nonesuch."

Search the village and you'll find the Nonesuch sign, which once stood beside the highway, now attached to the brick wall of the firehouse.

I suppose it is safe there from vandals and souvenir hunters, but I am troubled that many travelers to Nonesuch may never know the pleasure of being greeted by that wonderful place name that says so much about itself.

Surely, a total stranger could discern in the name Nonesuch a welcoming air of friendliness and wit. The same with Butterfly in Perry County, Blue Moon in Floyd, Rabbit Hash in Boone, Bearwallow in Barren and Hart, and Monkey's Eyebrow in Ballard.

Most of the settlements were named by early postmasters who either had vivid imaginations or who, pressed for a post office name that no one else had thought of, submitted the first idea that came to mind. When the Postal Service began closing many small post offices in recent years, the accompanying place names gradually began to fade from the landscape.

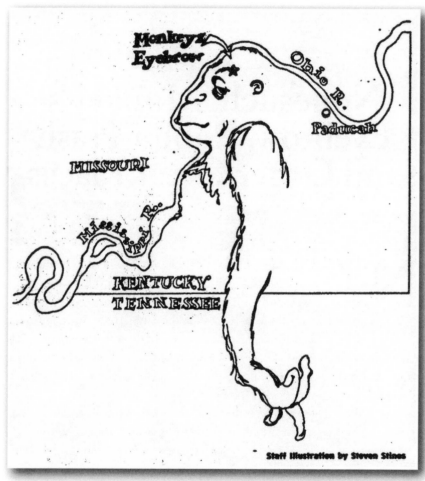

Staff Illustration by Steven Stines

There are numerous theories about how Monkey's Eyebrow got its name, none very plausible. And even Kentucky's place name experts admit they don't know. My theory is illustrated in artist Steven Stines' map with this story. Notice the shape of the Kentucky shoreline around Ballard County, how it resembles the head of a monkey. If you drew an eyebrow where one should be, it would be located exactly at Monkey's Eyebrow.

Identities were further diluted when scores of community schools which bore the same names as post offices were closed through school consolidation.

"The edge of town is now fuzzy," said Louisvillian Grady Clay, retired editor and current columnist for Landscape Architecture magazine, and now the weekly commentator for "Crossing the American Grain" on local public radio.

"It used to be, and still is in some cases, that you'd go across open country and suddenly, bing, there you were in a little town," Clay said. "But in the majority of the places I go, no longer suddenly does town stop and open fields begin, but you run down kind of a slow accretion of lots and houses strung out along the road, so that you're not sure whether you've come to the edge of town or not."

Should not that make the preservation of place names all the more imperative?

"Signing yourself is a crucial matter, whether you're signing a bank check or a will, or putting a sign out by the road," Clay said. "I am surprised at a report that I got from a friend at the University of Georgia that small towns in the South are not signing themselves. I would expect, but I don't have much evidence yet, that small towns, fearing a loss of identity, would multiply their signs."

The trouble with many of Kentucky's best place names, such as New York in Ballard County and Wild Cat in Clay, is that their signs have been stolen as souvenirs almost as soon as they were posted.

Highway officials rightfully argue that the signs are too expensive to keep replacing indefinitely. But without the signs will the places cease to be places and fade into the suburban fuzz that is eating away at the identities of many communities?

"The shutting out of yesterday is a preoccupation with a lot of people," Clay said. "A prime example is U.S. 127, where a whole bunch of lovely, wonderful little one-street towns have been bypassed by the 'new and improved' Highway 127; Swallowfield, Hustonville, Salvisa."

"The highway cuts through the countryside and overlays it rather than negotiating with it. I think if you look at the states touched by Highway 127, you're seeing a gradual shrinking of roadside society; a shrinking, shriveling and sterilizing."

Cow Creek National Bank

April 20, 1983

S ALYERSVILLE, Ky. – Unless you've lived in Magoffin County, you may never have heard of the Cow Creek National Bank.
That is unless you happened to have been employed by one of the many supply houses which, on the strength of the bank's letters of credit, sold untold thousands of dollars worth of wholesale goods to nonexistent businesses on Cow Creek around 1920, give or take a few years.

The Cow Creek National Bank, you see, was one of Eastern Kentucky's truly legendary swindles, for the bank and, for that matter, the businesses to which it extended credit, existed only on paper.

Cow Creek itself is not much more than a wet-weather branch that ripples out of the sleepy hillsides of west-central Magoffin County and eventually marries up with the Licking River.

The community was inhabited in those days by folks who, though lacking in formal education, possessed an incredible shrewdness when it came to horse trading.

To this day, no one seems quite sure who masterminded the Cow Creek National Bank scheme. And not many folks in Magoffin County are willing to discuss what they've heard of the swindle, for fear of incriminating surviving participants or embarrassing their families.

So I have pieced the story together as best I can, from what has been told to me by several dependable sources, some of whom were familiar with participants in the swindle, and from an old article written by Albert K. Moore in the Salyersville Independent.

According to Ollie Arnett, a lifelong resident of Magoffin County and reputable Salyersville businessman, one of the principals in the swindle was a local notary public who always rode a fine horse and carried pockets full of fountain pens and important looking papers.

He often prepared income-tax forms, Arnett said, and was frequently known to dispense with the paperwork and send the Internal Revenue Service a simple letter stating:

"John Jones is enclosing a check for $50. He said that he made about $3,000 last year. If the enclosed amount in not sufficient, etc. etc."

The bank's checks and stationery were supposedly the work of a notorious dog trader on Cow Creek, recognized as one of the finest scribes in that part of the country. Indeed, it is said that the name of a dog was even listed on the bank letterhead as one of its officers.

"They had a stamp or a seal of some kind that they could write a certified check," said Rube Reed, 71, a former Magoffin County sheriff who is now retired and living in the Cow Creek area.

There were at least six or seven people involved in the swindle, and perhaps more, Reed believes.

One of them was thought to have been postmaster for a time at Stella, the address listed for the Cow Creek National Bank.

The scheme involved placing large orders for food, dry goods, appliances and anything else the crooks could think of with large supply houses in other states.

The orders—in the names of phony businesses in the vicinity of Cow Creek—were accompanied by appropriate letters of credit from the bank.

Shippers were instructed to send the goods by rail to train stations at nearby Adel, Royalton or Jackson.

The merchandise was picked up there by the businessmen and carted away. It then was sold for whatever price could be gotten. And often it was given away.

"People in the community knew what they were doing," Reed said. "They'd give you half the stuff they ordered, if you'd haul it away. I remember going over there to the rail station with my dad to get a load of flour."

One time, Reed recalls, a load of glass doors came in, and shortly thereafter it seemed that half the people in Magoffin County had glass doors in their houses.

Another shipment consisted of a load of men's hats, which were sold at whatever price was offered.

When the companies that had been victimized had problems collecting their money, they finally sent letters to the authorities at Stella asking that legal action be taken.

These were intercepted by the postmaster and, in due time, were answered on beautiful "City of Stella" stationery from someone identifying himself as a judge.

The judge informed the company that he had collected the account and would send them the money after he had received the proper 15 percent commission and $10 court costs.

In the meantime, merchandise continued to roll into Cow Creek.

Electric washing machines showed up on many porches in the county years before there was any electricity available. And the story goes that a steam engine arrived C.O.D. one day and sat for months at the rail station.

Reed says that a large boat was even shipped on two flatcars. It was so big that it could not be unloaded and had to be returned.

Moore wrote in the Independent that a long investigation by postal inspectors finally resulted in the prosecution of some of the Cow Creek swindlers, each of whom was reportedly sent to prison for one year for using the mails to defraud.

To this day, most Magoffin County residents believe that the ringleaders of the scheme were never caught.

And it is said that for years after the swindle, many businesses in Magoffin County could order merchandise only after they paid cash in advance.

ILLUSTRATION BY B. CRAWFORD

Lion Attack

October 12, 2003

BROUGHTONTOWN, Ky. – When Arthur Genton heard news reports last week that a tiger had nearly killed famous illusionist Roy Horn of the entertainment team Siegfried & Roy, he had a brief flashback to his own near-death experience with a big cat two decades earlier.

Genton was attacked by his 450-pound pet lioness, Mindy, in June 1983, and was hospitalized for a week.

"I had the cat chained in the yard and was putting her in for the evening, but she was wanting to play instead of going in her pen," he said. "My brother-in-law was there and said, 'If we take her food into the pen, maybe she'll go in.' He went and picked it up, and she didn't like that."

When the lioness jumped up on Genton with her front paws, as she often did when the two were playing, he noticed that she was unusually agitated and that her approximately two-inch-long claws, resting on his shoulders, were now extended instead of retracted for the first time he could remember.

"She scratched my arm and I started bleeding pretty much," Genton said.

"She got back down on the ground and some of my blood was running down my arm. I guess she got a taste of that blood and thought it was pretty good, and she couldn't stop."

Genton's wife, Jean, who witnessed the episode, remembers the lioness

Arthur Genton walked with Mindy in December 1982, about six months before the lioness attacked him.

making a strange growling sound that she had never heard before as the animal began chewing on Arthur's arms and hands. Her husband, who is six feet tall, was at least a head shorter than the lioness when her paws were on his shoulders.

"I had never seen her that close on Arthur for that long a time," Jean Genton said. "It seemed like five minutes, but he had always told me not to make any sudden moves, so I was just peeping around a tree, watching. He got this strange expression on his face, and it finally got to the point where he told us we were going to have to shoot her, or whatever, to get her off of him."

Genton's brother-in-law found a rifle and shot the lioness. The wounded animal ran away and soon died.

"By the time Genton reached a hospital some 20 miles away," Jean Genton said, "his hands were swollen to twice their normal size." She later counted more than 70 puncture wounds on his left arm and hand, and numerous other punctures and claw marks on his right arm, upper body, and legs.

Genton, 47, a builder and designer of the .50-caliber Viper rifle and owner of Genton Tool & Die in Lincoln County, still has a few scars from the attack. He bought the animal from a woman in Mercer County about two years earlier. She had acquired the lioness as a youngster from a zoo in Wisconsin, but had later been advised by her attorney to get rid of the animal because of potential dangers. Genton has never owned another large, exotic animal.

"If someone hadn't intervened, I have no doubt she would eventually have gone ahead and killed me," he said. "My advice to anybody who wants a pet like that is to have security with them at all times."

Jesse and Frank James' Parents Married Here

August 23, 2002

S TAMPING Ground, Ky. – The Scott County home where outlaws Jesse and Frank James' parents were married will get its own Kentucky highway historical marker tomorrow.

The circa 1790s home, located on Locust Fork Pike, just north of Stamping Ground, is the former residence of James M. Lindsay, an uncle and guardian of Zerelda Cole, who was the mother of Jesse and Frank James.

The parlor mantel before which Cole and Robert James took their wedding vows in December 1841 is still standing.

Both bride and groom were children of well-to-do, respected families in Scott and Woodford counties. Robert James was, at the time, a student of the Baptist ministry at nearby Georgetown College, from which he later graduated.

"The provost and dean of the college, Dr. William Pollard, will be bringing greetings from Georgetown College at the program Saturday," said Ann Bevins, Scott County Historical Markers chairwoman. "And I understand that, although he can't be at the program, Dr. William Crouch, the president of the college, has a lot of fun with the fact that the father of the two outlaws was a graduate of Georgetown."

James Sames of Versailles, a genealogist whose great-great-grandmother was a sister of Jesse and Frank James' father, will be among a few James relatives who are expected at the unveiling of the roadside marker.

Although Robert and Zerelda James moved to Missouri in 1842, where Frank and Jesse were born in 1843 and 1847, the family kept close ties with Kentucky relatives and friends.

"Jesse and Frank visited back here all the time," Sames said. He has documentation that the brothers visited nearby relatives during their outlaw years after the Civil War. And he believes it is likely they visited the home where their parents were married and which was occupied by their relatives for several generations.

John Waymond Barber, 70, of Stamping Ground, whose family traces a distant connection with the Jameses and who donated the highway marker, bought the home in 1999.

"I'd always loved the old place for years, and found my opportunity to buy it," Barber said. "The house has eight rooms, four of them log."

He's been told that one of Zerelda Cole's grandmothers died upstairs in the house.

PHOTO BY BYRON CRAWFORD

Kentucky's Flag Man

April 13, 2007

RANKFORT, Ky. – The miniature Kentucky flag resting on the corner of Taylor Davidson's desk in his Frankfort workshop was a gift from a secretary 45 years ago.

Davidson, 88, a retired brigadier general, was then an assistant to the adjutant general of Kentucky and was reorganizing the Kentucky National Guard.

While ordering Kentucky flags for the units, he noticed the flag designs varied noticeably among suppliers.

"Sometimes the flag showed a farmer being embraced by a city slicker; sometimes it was a guy in knickers being embraced by somebody else," Davidson said. "And I said, 'I've got to do something about this and get some kind of standard.'"

In 1961 Davidson and Adjutant General A.Y. Lloyd named a committee to work on a design based on previous flags.

Eugenia Blackburn, of the Kentucky Historical Society, and Frankfort artist Harold Collins, who had painted portraits of several governors, were among those appointed. Davidson began digging through records back to the late 1700s.

Kentucky had briefly flown the Virginia flag after the Revolutionary War, then the flag of 15 stars and stripes after being admitted to the Union, then variations on several battle flags during the Civil War.

"I asked Collins to make a line sketch of what we had concluded to be

the authentic Kentucky flag,"
Davidson said. "The general
thought it was fine, and we
brought it to the attention of
the governor (Bert Combs),
and he thought it was fine."

In 1962, the committee
settled on a frontiersman
dressed in buckskins greet-
ing a man dressed in a suit
reminiscent of 19th-century
fashions. It symbolized the
link between frontier Kentuckians and later business
and industrial pioneers.

Statutes adviser Charles
Wheeler and Davidson com-
posed a statute, approved by
the legislature, requiring that

PHOTO BY BYRON CRAWFORD

the state flag be "of Navy blue silk, nylon, wool or cotton bunting, or some
other suitable material, with the seal of the Commonwealth encircled by
a wreath, the lower half of which shall be goldenrod in bloom and the
upper half the words 'Commonwealth of Kentucky.'"

The dimensions of the flag may vary, "but the length shall be 1.9 times
the width, and the diameter of the seal and encirclement shall be approximately two-thirds the width of the flag."

Davidson's favorite part reads:

"The emblem at the head of a flagstaff used to display the flag of the
Commonwealth of Kentucky shall be the Kentucky cardinal in an alert
but restful pose, cast in bronze, brass or other suitable material."

"The cardinal never caught on," he said.

Davidson, a Clay County native and University of Kentucky graduate,
served as both deputy adjutant general and state director of Selective Service before retirement. He and his wife, Bobbie, remained in Frankfort.

Many of his friends are unaware of his history with the flag, and most
still call him "Colonel," a rank he held for several years with the Kentucky
Air National Guard.

Ed Spilly, a Louisville collector of hunting and fishing gear, said Davidson is now better known for his skills in building and restoring fine bamboo flyrods, repairing casting reels, fishing equipment and sewing machines than for his designs of the Kentucky flag.

But when General Davidson is occasionally asked to tell the story of the Kentucky flag, he always takes the time.

"You've got to be known for something," he said.

Racing History

April 14, 2000

MIDWAY, Ky. – In a rolling pasture on the Nantura Stock Farm in Woodford County, beneath a peaceful grove of old locusts and hackberries, rest what some racing historians believe may be America's oldest grave markers for thoroughbreds.

One of the two 19th-century markers bears the name Longfellow; the other, Ten Broeck.

Time has blurred the epitaphs with lichens, but all the words are still visible. One marker of gray granite reads: "LONGFELLOW, The King of the Turf, brown horse, foaled May 10th, 1867, died November 5th, 1893. 17 starts ... 14 times first. King of Racers and King of Stallions."

A nearby Italian marble marker reads: "TEN BROECK, bay horse, folded (foaled) on Nantura Stock Farm, Woodford Co. Ky., June 29th, 1872. Died June 28th, 1887." A list of his performances is carved on the marker - from 1 mile up to 4 miles.

They were grand horses - Longfellow and Ten Broeck - bred, owned and trained by John Harper with help from his nephew, Frank Harper, who helped make Nantura a prominent stable in the 1870s and 1880s. Poems and songs were written about the Harpers and their horses.

Frank Harper's obituary in The Courier-Journal in April 1905 noted, "Mr. Harper loved Ten Broeck and Longfellow with affection as deep and tender as though they were human. When they died, they were buried with honors on a choice plat of bluegrass within view of his dwelling, and their resting places were marked with handsome and imposing monuments ... Frank Harper was the first man in America, as far as is known, to place a monument over the grave of a horse."

Six decades later, The Blood-Horse magazine would describe Longfellow as "beyond question the most celebrated horse of the 1870s." His exceptional length at birth had earned him the name Longfellow, and he grew to be one of the tallest colts in the Bluegrass at 17 hands.

Longfellow was born eight years before the Kentucky Derby began and never had a chance to run in that great race. But by age 4 he was considered the best horse of the year, beating both Milt Sanford's 4-year-old Preakness and August Belmont's Kingfisher over distances of more than two miles, and earning the sobriquet "King of the Turf."

Although his stable mate, Ten Broeck, ran fifth to Aristides in the first Kentucky Derby in 1875, and lost again to Aristides as a 4-year-old, Ten Broeck won 18 of his next 19 starts through age six. He broke several American records, including the time for distances of 2 miles and 3 miles - one week apart. At Churchill Downs, he shaved almost four seconds off the American record for 4 miles with his time of 7:15.

Today, Nantura Stock Farm raises cattle, tobacco, and hay. But its owners, Marlin and June Mitchell, whose family acquired the farm in 1972 from a descendant of the Harpers, share a deep respect for its rich and colorful racing past. Marlin Mitchell has erected black plank fences

around the two grave markers to prevent cattle from damaging the stones, and he patiently shares the story of the markers with occasional visitors to the site.

Mitchell is not certain that the Nantura monuments are the oldest markers in the country, but so far, he says, no one has proved otherwise.

"Until I hear someone telling me there's one older than these, I'll believe these are the oldest," he said.

69

Derby Cat

April 9, 1993

SHELBYVILLE, Ky. – A private pre-Derby tradition of mine is that of going to George Pigg's Barber Shop in Shelbyville and listening to George tell the story of his yellow tomcat named Derby. Since I first heard the story several years ago, I have been drawn back to the little shop each year about this time to hear it again. I ask that George spare no details as he parks himself in the front chair, lights a cigarette, looks out toward the street with a pained countenance, and begins the story. The words roll out, riding on little puffs of smoke. "It all started in 1979," George says. "My sister was in here from California, and on Derby Day we were all outside, and this little yellow cat came up to the house. I didn't want a cat, but my sister said, 'Oh, George, why don't you keep that cat? It's so lovable.'

"It was Derby Day, so we named him Derby."

Spectacular Bid won the Kentucky Derby that afternoon, and Derby the cat won George Pigg's affection. For many months thereafter, every day was Derby day, you might say.

George, who has been barbering nearly 32 years, remembers that as soon as he pulled in the driveway most afternoons, Derby would be waiting on the sidewalk, rolling and purring, waiting to play. At night, he sometimes lay on George's lap as they watched TV or read.

"He was the most lovable cat you've ever seen, and sharp as a tack," George says.

Then one Friday in the spring, about two years after he had arrived, Derby vanished without a trace. George's heart sank the following Sunday morning when he saw the lifeless body of a yellow cat beside U.S. 60 on the eastern edge of Shelbyville.

"It was raining so hard you couldn't hardly see to do anything, but I pulled over and got out and turned the cat over and looked at him to make sure ... and I said, 'That's Derby.'"

He set about the grim task of moving Derby back to his place for burial.

"It was still just pouring down rain when I got back and went to put the cat in a sack," George says. "That was about the time church was out, and I was there getting that cat, and everybody driving along was slowing down, looking and waving at me. You've never seen such awful looks in your life. I could just see what they were thinking – 'What in the hell is George Pigg doing out there picking up a dead cat in a downpour?'"

Though soaked to the bone, George dug a hole near his house and gave the cat a proper burial as soon as he got home.

"I had a ceremony and said a little prayer for him."

Six weeks later, George looked up one day to see the real Derby walking through the yard toward the house, tired and gaunt but very much alive.

"I was dumbfounded," he says. "I just buried the wrong cat."

Derby lived about six more years, and finally died of natural causes.

ILLUSTRATION BY WIEDERWOHL

Air Force Academy Fly-By

September 23, 1987

NICHOLASVILLE, Ky. – Did you know that Central Kentucky and Southern Indiana were once considered as potential sites for the Air Force Academy?

In April 1954, the Air Force Academy Site Selection Commission, which included legendary aviator Charles A. Lindbergh, toured a 9,700-acre tract near Shakertown in Mercer County, and a 15,000-acre site near the Kentucky River in Jessamine County.

The five-member commission then inspected sites just down the Ohio River from Madison, Indiana, and across the river in Trimble County, Ky.

It is forgotten history now to all but a few such as Esther Cannon, a Jessamine County historian, and Elesteen Hager, 78, a Nicholasville funeral director who was Lindbergh's chauffeur during the visit.

"I guess the chamber of commerce here called me because, being in the funeral business, we had a limousine," said Hager, who served in the state legislature for many years. "So I went to the Lexington airport and picked up Lindbergh, and we made the rounds."

Hager said Lindbergh was the only member of the commission he remembers seeing on the one-day Central Kentucky tour.

"He was just nice and easy to talk to; not a show off, just as humble as could be," Hager said.

At the time, Lindbergh was a brigadier general in the Air Force Reserve.

"As I understood it, just in conversation with him, he was going from here to the spot where they finally made the decision to locate the academy," outside Colorado Springs, Colorado, Hager said.

Courier-Journal files contain only two stories about the site searches in the region; one detailing the visits to the Bluegrass area, and another about Southern Indiana and Trimble County.

The accounts quote Merrill C. Meigs, vice president of the Hearst Corp. in Chicago and spokesman for the

Hager holds a photo of Lindbergh during the visit to Central Kentucky.

site selection commission, as saying that his group had "many more sites to inspect" before deciding, but that the scenery in the Bluegrass region "is even more attractive than I have heard it described."

In Southern Indiana, the commission encountered some protests to their visit at Saluda, a small community within the site area.

"Go back to Madison, Don't Take Our School, Save Saluda," read one crudely painted cardboard sign stretched across a road.

"We're proud people around here," one Saluda resident said. "We don't have too much, but we don't want to be run off from what we do have."

They weren't. Two months later, the Air Force chose 15,000 acres just north of Colorado Springs, touching off what was called "a billion dollar boom" in the city, which had a population of 52,000 then. About 215,000 people live there now.

The site selection commission, unable to agree on one site, had recommended three sites to the Secretary of the Air Force. The other two sites were not disclosed.

Hensley Settlement

September 23, 1998

MIDDLESBORO, Ky. – Visitors emerge from the forest on top of Brush Mountain along the Kentucky-Virginia border into a clearing of rolling meadows and quaint log farmsteads where no one lives.

Hensley Settlement in Bell County was deserted in 1951 when Sherman Hensley - who in 1903 had become the first of his clan to settle there - became the last to leave.

Since then the abandoned settlement has fascinated thousands who have visited Cumberland Gap National Park in which the secluded settlement is located.

"One thing that makes the place so unusual is the isolation," said National Park Service Ranger Jack Collier.

"Another is the exposure. It's sitting up there at 3,200-feet elevation, right on top of a mountain. The men would come off the mountain some, but it was a rare thing indeed if the one of the women got to come off the mountain."

Even today the only road to the settlement is a narrow gravel trail four-and-a-half miles long up the side of the mountain. Most visitors ride Park Service vehicles to the mountaintop, but a few hike to the settlement from the Cumberland Gap pinnacle, eight miles away, or over steep terrain from Chadwell Gap, Va., three miles away.

Here, among the surviving dozen or so homes and outbuildings left by the Hensleys and their kinfolk, the Gibbonses, visitors try to imagine what life must have been like on the mountain when the population neared 100 and the settlement had 40 buildings.

The Hensleys acquired 500 acres there from a family named Bales in the spring of 1903. The land was later subdivided into 16 small farms that had about 200 tillable acres.

Each family usually planted a large garden, grew hay and corn, and raised livestock. After the fall harvest, people cleared land.

The Hensley Settlement in Cumberland Gap National Park was settled by the Hensley family about 1903. The area is located atop 3,200-foot Brush Mountain.

Snows often came early and heavy, and fog sometimes hung over the fields until late in the morning. No road and no electricity ever reached the settlement while it was occupied.

"For the most part ... cows and hogs stayed fat on whatever was in the woods," Collier said. "Back then, they had a lot of chestnuts in the fall of the year, and they'd get good and fat."

The Park Service has restored the one-room Brush Mountain School, which may have once had about 45 students.

Ranger Matthew Graham often shares with visitors the story of a young teacher at the school, Stella Callahan, who stole the heart of one of the Hensley boys who was a student of hers but nearly as old as she. He proposed marriage, she accepted, and the wedding took place right there at the school - which also served as the settlement's church.

Willie Gibbons was the settlement's blacksmith and furniture maker. He made the coffins for many of those who are buried under fieldstone markers in the Hensley Cemetery.

After World War II, people began leaving the settlement. Some left to find jobs. Others married outsiders who didn't want to live on the mountain. Eventually, only Sherman Hensley was left, and he finally sold out to the Park Service. He died in the spring of 1979 and is buried on the mountain where he spent most of his life.

Each August, many Hensley and Gibbons descendants return to Brush Mountain to walk again among the empty log buildings and paling fences that stand as a memorial to their family's pioneer spirit.

Last Stagecoach
Out of Kentucky

February 25, 1991

BURNSIDE, Ky. – Wells Fargo Bank of San Francisco has assured the small town of Burnside that the Burnside-Monticello Stage-coach—the last one that operated in Kentucky—is safe and sound and still drawing sightseers to the bank's museum in Los Angeles.

Wells Fargo, which gained fame as a stagecoach line in the Old West and whose bank now has approximately 520 branch offices in California, paid $85,000 for the nine-passenger coach in 1979.

The coach ran for a short time between Columbia and Campbellsville during the late 1890s. But from 1901 until at least the summer of 1912, it carried passengers, mail and freight between the Southern Kentucky towns of Burnside and Monticello along the Cumberland River. Some historians claim that it was still operating in 1915 and that it was not only the last to operate in Kentucky, but also the last one east of the Mississippi River.

Its owner and operator during those years, Charles H. Burton, died in 1923, and his son, John C. Burton of Monticello, kept the old red coach until his death in 1973.

In 1977, the Kentucky Court of Appeals intervened in a dispute among Burton's relatives over ownership of the antique vehicle. As a result, the near-mint-condition, 2,300-pound stagecoach, which had been stored in a barn for half a century, was sold at auction on the courthouse steps in Monticello

on July 29, 1979, to settle
the disagreement.

Kenneth Ballou, a funeral director from Burkesville, bought it for $38,750. He sold it to Wells Fargo five months later for $85,000, which, at the time, was believed by collectors to be the highest price ever paid for a stagecoach in the United States.

The coach was built in 1895 by the Abbott-Downing Co. of Concord, NH, a builder of some of the finest coaches of that day, including most of the Wells Fargo stages. The coach was bought new for $2,000 in 1897 by J.B. Barbee of Columbia.

COURIER-JOURNAL ARCHIVES

Responding to a recent inquiry by the city of Burnside concerning the whereabouts and condition of the coach, Wells Fargo Museum spokeswoman Elaine Gillerman said from San Francisco last week that the refurbished coach is one of seven or eight original coaches that the company owns and exhibits at the Wells Fargo Museum at 333 S. Grand Ave. in Los Angeles.

Wells Fargo has promised to send Burnside an 8-by-10 picture of the coach for a scrapbook about its history that local historian Bernice Mitchell has compiled and donated to the city.

"All we've asked for is a picture of it in its final resting place," said Elizabeth Brooks, the clerk-treasurer of Burnside. "I think that would be a final page in our scrapbook—from the beginning to end."

Footnote: A spokesperson for the Wells Fargo Museum in Los Angeles said in 2009 that the stage was still on exhibit and was the museum's "pride and joy."

Santa Train

December 24, 2006

S HELBYVILLE, Ky. – Many Christmases before the screen adaptation of Chris Van Allsburg's seasonal classic "The Polar Express," Esther Jo Long lived her own small version of the magical children's story as a 5-year-old.

During the late 1930s and early '40s, she and her parents, James and Mabel Morris, her three sisters and one brother lived in a large old farmhouse beside the L & N Railroad tracks on the northern outskirts of Shelbyville. Her father was a tobacco farmer.

"I was the baby of the family," she said. "We weren't what I would consider poor, but I didn't know at the time that we were kind of strapped for money."

One day while her mother was hanging clothes on the line in the backyard and Esther Jo was playing nearby, an engineer waved to her as the big steam locomotive rumbled past, and Esther Jo waved back.

Soon, she was waving to other engineers and to conductors on the freights and passenger trains that passed every day.

"As things continued, they started throwing me off small items; a bag of candy, chewing gum, comic books or toys, nearly once a week," she said. "Even when I wasn't at home, we would sometimes come back home and there would be a little bundle of something out on the bank that they had thrown to me while I was away.

To a small child it was just fantastic."

Once when the train was stopped at the crossing nearby, an engineer with a long gray beard helped her into the engine and let her sit at the controls of the locomotive and wave to her mother. The engineer was J. J. Allen, who lived in Winchester, Ky.

C.L. Love of Danville, 88, who served more than 40 years as a conductor for the Norfolk Southern Railway, recalls that he and other trainmen often pitched treats and small gifts to children who waved to them along the Southern tracks. Grown-ups who lived near the railroad often looked forward to newspapers that the trainmen pitched from windows of the passing trains.

Esther Jo

"We'd take stuff from home sometimes" to throw off, Love said.

The bookmark moment of Esther Jo's friendship with the trainmen came on a snowy Christmas morning when she was about 5. She was upset that the snow was so deep that she could not go out in the yard to wave. But when she heard the train coming, her mother raised the window on the side of the house next to the tracks, and Esther Jo leaned out to wave through the snowflakes.

"We noticed that the train was slowing down and slowing down and when it got right to our side yard, the conductor stepped down on the very last step and dropped this big box for me. Of course I just nearly had a fit when I saw him do that," she remembered.

"My dad went out and waded through the snow and brought it in for me. It was a big doll with a long, white dress and a bonnet on. I would say it was probably 24 to 30 inches long, just a beautiful doll. The note said, 'From your railroad friends.' Of course I just cherished that doll."

A few years later the doll and nearly all of the family's other possessions were lost when their home beside the tracks was destroyed by fire. But Esther Jo Long's vivid memories of that distant, snowy Christmas morning, and the kindness of the trainmen to a little girl who stood in the yard and waved have never dimmed.

"It's just something that has stuck with me all my life," she reflected. "To this day, I just absolutely love trains ... and if I have a chance I will still wave to a trainman wherever I am."

Murray State's Shoe Tree

May 12, 1993

MURRAY, Ky. – A tattered string on a weather-beaten Reebok stirs in the soft spring breeze around the "shoe tree" on the campus of Murray State University. Moss grows on the toe of a man's loafer, curled with age and hanging all alone.

The worn-out shoes nailed to the sugar maple are scarcely noticed by students rushing past on their way to final exams. Dozens of shoes of various descriptions have been left over the years by students who gave their hearts to each other at Murray State, and who each left one shoe nailed beside the other's as tokens to the entire campus that they were sole mates forever, or something like that. "All I know is that if you meet somebody here and you eventually marry, you get your shoe up on the tree with them," said Joanna Hendrick, a freshman from Salem, Ill.

At last count, there were approximately 50 shoes on the tree. But there are also many empty nails, suggesting that, in time, some of the shoes have rotted away or maybe, as one passing student jokingly surmised, been borrowed by financially pressed students who needed footwear.

Some students are skeptical that all the shoes left on the tree belong to married couples. They quietly hint that a few pairs of shoes commemorate only some very torrid romances. In any case, dozens of loves have been pledged on the tree over the last 30 years.

Bob McGaughey, chairman of Murray's journalism department, remembers a few shoes being placed on the tree when he was a student at

81

the school in the early 1960s. "Somebody had put three or four shoes on the tree, and nobody knew why they were there. But I think couples started putting them up there about '65 or '66," he said. "There have been some funny ones, where people put them up there as kind of a joke, like the largest shoe they could find, then a little bitty shoe, and people would say, 'What kind of couple was that?'"

The names and dates scribbled with markers on many of the shoes remain legible. Joeli's sneaker is stuffed inside Alan's. "Jeff & Nekayah, May 27, 1989," climbed into the forks of the sugar maple to leave their shoes. "David and Lena" tied their shoes together with a double knot after nail-

At the time of this story there were approximately 50 shoes nailed onto the trunk and some limbs of the special tree at Murray State University.

PHOTO BY BYRON CRAWFORD

ing them to the tree. Psychology majors at Murray State could have a field day analyzing the tree.

What is to be inferred from the inscription "Oops!" on Paul's sneaker? What is the meaning of a man's shoe tongue nailed to the tree all alone? Where is the woman who married the man whose designer loafer had a shiny silver star on the toe? And what of the woman whose shoe was attached, not with the customary nail, but with a thumb tack?

Perhaps there are no answers, but the questions are blowing in the wind – in the strings that dangle from the shoe tree on the campus of Murray State University.

Footnote: The original MSU Shoe Tree was destroyed by a storm several years after this story was written, but another shoe tree was established in the same line of trees nearby.

A Shocking Film

July 22, 1981

B AGDAD, Ky. – Nearly five years have passed since I first heard this story. I have spent those years considering how best to tell it. The setting is the rural Shelby County farming settlement of Bagdad where, by coincidence, I now live.*

There is not usually much excitement here, save the whistle of an occasional passing freight train. But one summer night nearly fifty years ago there was excitement enough to last a while.

It was during the mid-to-late 1930s, most agree, on a weeknight they're pretty sure, and a good sized crowd had gathered in the middle of town. A large white tarpaulin was hung on the side of a boxcar, and nearby a movie projector was set up, its electrical cord stretching along the ground to an outlet at the pool hall.

The town was abuzz with activity. Merchants had struck upon a novel idea for attracting customers. They sponsored the showing of free movies one night a week, and because Bagdad had no movie theater, the films were shown outdoors.

Already, the open-air picture shows had become extremely popular, and some estimate that there may have been 300 people in town that night, well above Bagdad's population.

Most folks drove their automobiles to the movie showings, and parked them on the edges of town in all directions. A few people walked, of course, and some rode or drove horses.

Certainly Annie Grigsby drove a horse, for her animal is a central figure in this story. He was uncommonly ordinary, just an old black horse,
good for farm work and for pulling Mrs. Grigsby's surrey into Bagdad for
the weekly picture shows.

On this night he was smack-dab in the middle of things, standing a little left of the projector. Mrs. Grigsby, and possibly others,
were seated in the surrey, and a host of men, women and children
were gathered around to watch a western picture starring Hopalong
Cassidy. Liar's benches had been pulled from storefronts for seating.
Some people had brought chairs or lard cans from home. Others sat
on empty cream cans they had borrowed from the railroad loading
dock a few feet away.

Everybody who was anybody around Bagdad was there, and a few who
weren't.

The picture show began with the usual signs on the screen, naming
merchants who were sponsoring the movie, and then, I suppose, Hopalong Cassidy thundered across the tarpaulin and a hush fell over the
crowd, because they all loved a western.

Mrs. Grigsby's old horse was quiet, too, except that flies were bothering
him and he stomped his feet occasionally. The plot thickened. Hopalong
was hot on some outlaw's trail, or they were hot on his. It was about time
for the film to break, which generally happened a few times during every
show. But no, the film held, and oddly enough, no one even remembers
a train coming through that night, as they always seemed to do, usually
drowning out the sound during the best part of the movie. Eyes were
fixed on Hopalong, and no one paid any mind to Mrs. Grigsby's horse,
which kept stomping at flies.

No one noticed that he was standing directly over the movie projector's
power cord, and that his persistent stomping had cut through the insula-
tion on that part of the power cord directly beneath his hind quarters.

It might all have been of little consequence, except for what happened
next. Without going into great detail, I'll simply say that the horse had
been well-watered before coming to the movie, and horses don't go looking for restrooms when it is time to go.

When water meets with electrical current, the charge usually follows
the stream to its source. Mrs. Grigsby's old black horse soon discovered
his ill-timed mistake, and could not stand still under the circumstances.

Reliable witnesses, and there were many, claimed that the poor old horse went straight up.

One woman said, "fire flew." The projector short-circuited and blew out. Mrs. Grigsby screamed for someone to hold the beast until she could depart the surrey. People scattered in all directions.

Riley Sleets, who had borrowed a cream can on which to sit and watch the movie, ran all the way home before realizing that he was carrying the can with him, and had to turn around and bring it back.

People ran under the box cars, over the tops of automobiles and over each other! Luckily, there were no serious injuries reported. The horse broke for the railroad tracks, but was apprehended before it got away. Otherwise, I suppose it would still be running.

 * *Footnote: Our family moved from Bagdad to nearby Shelbyville during the 1980s. People around town were still talking about the night the horse ran off with the movie.*

Belle's Bordello
Now A Soccer Locker

June 21, 1996

LEXINGTON, Ky. — That whirring noise you may have heard coming from Lexington lately might be the sound of Belle Brezing spinning in her grave.

What would the city's most famous madam say about the conversion of her original bordello into a women's locker room for such wholesome and unprofitable pursuits as women's college soccer and softball?

Brezing, who is widely believed to have been the inspiration for novelist Margaret Mitchell's character Belle Watling in "Gone with the Wind," operated a brothel on North Upper Street early in her career.

"The irony of it all is that it now is a women's locker room," said Transylvania University women's softball coach Sherry Holley. "I think it's sort of a neat thing. We've discussed it in a lighthearted way, and of course we have little jokes around the locker room about it being our brothel."

While most of the Transylvania women's softball team members are not familiar with Brezing's notorious place in Lexington's history, both Holley and assistant coach Sandy Duncan have explained the Brezing row house's significance to team members and to prospective recruits who visit the campus.

The full story of Brezing takes a while to tell. In the late 1800s and early 1900s she turned her talents for business, interior decorating and

86

"entertainment" into a highly successful, if disreputable, enterprise that catered to some of the elite of Bluegrass society.

Brezing soon amassed a small fortune, which allowed her to invest in stocks and real estate. She finally moved to a plush three-story mansion at Northeastern and Wilson avenues in Lexington, where "entertainers" were not allowed downstairs unless wearing an evening dress. Belle, always elegantly dressed, rode about the city in a handsome phaeton, drawn by a matched team of chestnuts.

When Brezing died at age 80, in the summer of 1940, Time magazine called her Lexington salon "the most orderly of disorderly houses."

Belle was laid to rest in Lexington's Calvary Cemetery, where several of the girls who had worked for her were also buried under an 8-foot-tall granite shaft inscribed: "Blessed be the pure in heart."

And now the house where Brezing started her first brothel is a modern locker room where young women wear cleats, uniforms and gloves.

Sometimes they are covered with dust. They get black eyes, sprained ankles and bloody noses, playing their hearts out for no pay.

If you hear a whirring sound, it may be Belle spinning again.

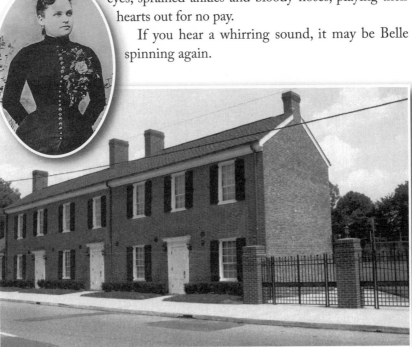

The renovated Belle Brezing house.

PART TWO:

Mysteries & Marvels

The Incredible Swiss Army Cap

November 17, 1996

D ON'T even bother trying to calculate the odds on this one, folks. Randy Acton of Elizabethtown is still shaking his head in amazement.

And Roger Nussbaumer of Santa Fe, N.M., was so shocked that he had to sit down when it happened.

Actually, the story began back in 1970 when Nussbaumer, then a member of the Swiss army, turned in his uniform in the city of Basel shortly before he came to the United States as a vice president of a laboratory-equipment company.

He eventually left that job and is now president of his own furniture-manufacturing business in New Mexico.

Some time ago his brother-in-law, a colonel in the Swiss army, visited Nussbaumer's home in Santa Fe and, while there, ordered some merchandise from U.S. Cavalry - a retail and mail-order chain based in Radcliff, Ky., that stocks thousands of items of military-surplus and adventure equipment.

Acton, U.S. Cavalry's president, travels all over the world buying surplus military equipment from foreign governments. In the spring of 1995, he made a large purchase from the Swiss army.

Because Nussbaumer's brother-in-law had his U.S. Cavalry order

BY ROGER NUSSBAUMER

shipped to Nussbaumer's home in New Mexico, Nussbaumer began receiving the U.S. Cavalry catalogs. One day as he was browsing through one he noticed some Swiss Alpine caps like the one he had worn during his years in the army.

"What I really wanted out of the catalog was a steel watch with a titanium coating, which I thought was a very good field watch," he said. "While I was on the phone ordering that, I thought, 'Well, for nostalgia purposes, I'm going to order an army coat and a rucksack,' and then I ordered three kinds of hats."

One of the caps was an older version like the one Nussbaumer's father had worn, one had a fleece lining, and the other was a simple gray wool garrison cap with the Swiss cross emblem, like the one Nussbaumer had turned in with his uniform 26 years earlier back in Switzerland.

"When the order was delivered and I opened the package I actually went right for the watch, because that was my primary purpose," Nussbaumer said. "I didn't even look at the rest until the following morning. But as I was looking over this merchandise, I saw that one of the caps had a name tag - and it hit me like that - 'R. Nussbaumer, Co. 3, Troop 1,' in my handwriting.

"I had to sit down. I looked at it. I stared at it. I tried to figure out whether it could be. There must be hundreds of thousands of these caps. It just became clear to me that…well, this is a very, very long shot…but that's the way it is. This is my hat."

What are the odds that a Swiss army veteran - out of service 26 years and living in New Mexico, 8,000 miles from where he turned in his uniform - would be sent his own army cap by a Kentucky military surplus mail-order company that shipped 600,000 orders and more than $45 million worth of equipment all over the world last year?

Acton says his company ordered 3,000 of the Swiss army caps, which were all in plastic bags and bar-coded. So it would have been almost impossible for anyone in the company to have matched Nussbaumer's cap with his name.

"We like to give good customer service," he said, "but we can't guarantee that this will ever happen again."

Roger Nussbaumer sported a Swiss Alpine cap of special significance.

Message in a Bottle

June 25, 2000

S the sun came up over Cuba one February day in 1997, Eredis
Gutierrez-Aguilera was fishing on a beach near his grandmother's house, when the Atlantic seaspray washed over a battered
wine bottle with a scrap of paper rolled up inside.

Eredis gently broke open the bottle and tried to read the yellowed
message. "There were some missing words, because they had been deleted
by the salty water, but in general I could understand what it said," recalled
Eredis, who now lives in Louisville. "On one side it said, 'Congratula-
tions, you have just found on the beach a note in a bottle.' On the other
side it had the description of this family (who set the bottle adrift); that
they lived on a rural farm in Minnesota, how many members of the family, their phone number and a blank space to fill out where the bottle was
found. They said it was released on Cape Cod, Martha's Vineyard, on July
30, 1993."

For Eredis Gutierrez-Aguilera, the message in a bottle was the answer
to many prayers.

The young medical student at Mariana Grajales University had been
praying for months that he would be granted permission to emigrate to
America, and now the message in a bottle that had washed up at his feet
from what seemed a world away filled him with new hope that he was
destined to live in the land beyond the Atlantic horizon.

He wrote the family who had released the bottle, the Lieskes, and

94

exchanged photographs. They added their prayers to his that he would be given permission to emigrate.

Several months later, the Cuban government allowed him to leave.

Now, Eridis, 24, his wife, Naillyvis, 23, and their one-year-old son, Eredis Jr., are living in a two bedroom, un-air-conditioned apartment on South Third Street in Louisville, while he works, often six nights a week, at a glass products company, and she works days as a hotel maid to make a new life in Kentucky.

LOUISVILLE COURIER-JOURNAL PHOTO

Eredis has been studying English at Jefferson Community College and hopes to one day enter medical school here to complete training to become a family physician. His wife, who speaks little English, also was in medical school in Cuba and plans to continue medical studies.

In the meantime, the two have applied for a visa to visit Cuba next month, where Eredis' father is ill and wants to see his grandson.

The June issue of Guideposts magazine features Eredis' story of the message of hope in a bottle and how it found him at a time when he most needed hope.

Eredis and Naillyvis spent their first Christmas in America in 1998 with Ron and Jayne Lieske and their four sons in the small town of Henderson, Minnesota, where they heard the Lieske's story of the bottle firsthand.

"We threw in seventeen bottles, I think, on that particular vacation. We were on a boat off Cape Cod," Ron Lieske said by phone last week. "A month or two later, we got a note back from some tuna fisherman up by Maine. All the bottles went north with the currents, but some branch into Ireland, England, down by Spain and around that way, then swing back up again by Cuba and the islands."

The bottle that came to rest at the feet of Eredis Gutierrez-Aguilera that morning in Cuba had been afloat for more than three-and-a-half years.

When Eredis and Naillyvis were finally cleared to go to the United States, they chose Louisville from a list of several cities where they might have been settled by Catholic charities, because they liked the description of Louisville as a place to work and raise a family.

"I would really like, if I can do something for the Spanish community here, to help them," Eredis said. "It's like something God inspired to let me come here."

Footnote: After this story appeared, a generous Louisville woman who was touched by the couple's determination sent them a check for $10,000. The couple became naturalized U.S. citizens in November 2003. Their two sons were born in this country. Fred is continuing to pursue a medical degree while working at a nursing home.

Snow Doughnuts

Winter, 1998

MOUNT STERLING, Ky. – Another winter is nearly gone and Tom Martin has all but given up hope of finding snow doughnuts again.

Twenty-one years have passed since he saw his first–and last–ones during the severe winter of 1977. One late January day he had gone to the local hospital to visit a friend when he overheard an elderly woman in the same hospital room tell of looking out the ambulance window on her way to the hospital and seeing large snow formations that looked like what she called, "doughnuts."

"At first I wondered what kind of medication she'd been taking, but in the purest of sciences you must believe first, then attempt to disprove," said Martin. "So I grabbed a camera and headed out toward Sharpsburg, and it wasn't long before I started seeing them in the fields."

Some were no larger than four to six inches in diameter. Others were perhaps a foot or more across. Martin theorizes that they had formed overnight when the wind raised a frozen layer of snow and rolled it into tubes. A strong wind coupled with rising temperatures the previous day and cold that evening had apparently created perfect conditions for the phenomenon. The next day, the snow doughnuts were gone.

Martin, 50, a writer-photographer and nationally known authority on the sport of rappelling, began searching for other winter phenomena after the snow doughnut experience. He found enough fascinating formations to literally fill a book.

His "Kentucky Ice," (Search Publishing) is an 80-page hardbound collection of photographs and descriptions of unusual ice and snow formations which were discovered during the winters of 1977, '78 and '79.

In addition to snow doughnuts, Martin also found a cave in Lee County in which nature had created a spectacular forest of hydromites, columns of ice that were formed by water dripping from the warmer cave ceiling into freezing air that swept along the cave floor, causing the ice columns to grow, drop-by-drop, until some were more than seven feet tall.

"There were thousands of them," Martin wrote. "There are no words to describe this place. My photographs do nothing to convey its mystery and beauty...I called it 'Cave of Heaven' because I assumed that this side of heaven I would never again see anything like it...

"The delicate columns of ice seem like crystal buildings in a crystal city, in a place found only in one's dreams. They take on an aura, a life, and knocking one down feels like killing something that is living."

Elsewhere around Eastern and Central Kentucky, Martin would find giant frozen waterfalls, small ice-draped plants of unique shapes and a fragile, scimitar shaped blade of ice which he described as, "perhaps the most exquisite piece of ice I have ever seen."

Each winter when Martin thinks conditions may be right for snow doughnuts, he searches the hills of Montgomery, Bath, Menifee, Wolfe and surrounding counties once again for the elusive creations. But they have never returned. Although hydromites still form in the cave most winters, they have never recurred in such numbers, or as tall, as during the winter of 1978.

Martin shares color slides of his ice discoveries each winter with students from elementary schools through college and with senior citizens' groups, encouraging them to look outside their back doors in winter for some of nature's most beautiful creations.

If they are lucky, maybe once in a lifetime, they will see a snow doughnut.

Footnote: After this story appeared in 1998, Steve Miller of Louisville wrote to say that he, too, had seen and photographed "snow doughnuts" while hiking in Wolfe County, about the same time Martin had seen them several miles away. Miller believes small whirlwinds may form the doughnuts from light, wet snow by creating hollow tubes of ice and snow.

Year Without A Summer

June 20, 1997

H AVE you ever heard of the year without a summer?" Kathryn Gokey of Louisville phoned to ask me last week.
 Her husband, Charles, remembered hearing the phrase somewhere, she said, but he couldn't remember the year or the circumstances.

Indeed, there was such a year, Mrs. Gokey - in 1816, when there were only 18 states, and very few weather records were being kept.

Within hours of your inquiry, my gifted team of field advisers had turned up a most interesting, undated, 250-word article titled "The Year 1816." It contains a detailed account of the so-called "year without a summer" in Indiana, which would become the 19th state in December 1816.

In his preface to the article, Kenneth Eck of the Purdue University Extension Service stated that a man named Cramer (first name unknown) had written the amazing account. Eck could not be reached to provide background on the story.

It states that "the second week of June (1816) snowstorms of one-to-nineteen inches covered 15 of the ...states and most of the territories ... that ponds and rivers froze every month that summer" and that in May, Indiana had snow or sleet a total of 17 days."

Farmers wore overcoats to plant their spring crops, the story goes. And there is a tale of one farmer who, while going to check on his sheep on June 17, jokingly told his family to call out the neighbors if he got lost in the snow. Soon after he left, he was trapped in a blizzard and both of his feet froze before he was found.

"The Hoosier 4th of July celebration was held in bitter weather ... August was even worse - more snow, frosts and blizzards."

Fish, wild game and wild plants kept many from starving. Wages diminished and inflation was rampant.

As incredible as the story sounds, Kentucky's state climatologist, Glen Conner of Western Kentucky University, confirms that 1816 was marked by winter-like conditions over much of the north and even as far south as Virginia.

Although Kentucky weather records date only to 1825, Conner assumes that the summer of 1816 in Kentucky that year was very cool.

"The previous year a volcano in Indonesia…had erupted, and the following year there was so much volcanic dust in the air that sunlight was having trouble getting through in quantities," Conner said.

"That year was called by the folk 'The Year Without A Summer' and also called 'Eighteen-hundred-and-froze-to-death.'"

Conner says a National Weather Service publication states that there were two snowfalls in New England during June of 1816, but he says the absence of good weather records in those pioneer days makes detailed documentation of 'the year without a summer' very difficult.

While 1997 certainly cannot be designated the "Year Without a Summer II," Conner says that, so far, it ranks among the top few years with daytime high temperatures below 75 degrees. Many are wondering what is causing the continued cool, rainy weather.

Although some weather watchers blame the extremes on El Niño - the atmospheric and oceanic circulation in the equatorial Pacific that affects weather in North America - Conner says he has seen no scientific data to suggest a direct connection between El Niño and Kentucky's current weather.

Speaking of extremes, Conner has in his files some interesting Kentucky weather facts regarding late snows and heavy rain.

On May 20, 1894, Springfield, Ky., received five inches of snow in a freak storm that visited only Washington County.

Weather observer Miles Saunders wrote that snow fell from 6 a.m. to noon and "went off in drizzling rain." He noted that trees broke under the weight of snow.

101

"Let me give you two gee-whizzes," Conner said.

"The least amount of rainfall that I know about in Kentucky was at Jeremiah in Letcher County in 1968 - 14.15 inches for the year. The most that I know about in a year was at Caneyville in Grayson County in 1979 - 88.07 inches."

Reel Secret

December 5, 1999

F RANKFORT, Ky. – When the Japanese bombed Pearl Harbor on Sunday, Dec. 7, 1941, all was quiet inside the George W. Gayle & Son fishing-reel shop on Logan Street near the Kentucky Capitol.

George W. Gayle, a watchmaker and jeweler, had started crafting precision bait-casting reels in the early 1880s, and his son, Clarence, had carried on his father's tradition of fine workmanship into the 1940s. Some of the Gayle reels in German silver fetched up to $300. But it was the flycasting reels that were produced in large quantities and often sold for as little as 50 cents that were the company's mainstay.

Clarence Gayle, a self-taught engineer, was an easygoing fisherman, but he took great pride in his work. He had been deeply disturbed in the 1930s when someone brought him a reel stamped "Geo. W. Gayle & Son, Frankfort, Ky.," on one side, and "Made in Japan" on the other. Adding insult to injury, the Japanese were selling the copies for less than Gayle could sell the real thing.

Slightly more than 10 years later, Gayle would help build the atomic bomb that brought Japan to its knees and ended World War II in 1945.

During the spring of 1943, he got a government contract to make some small parts for weapons.

"As the government contracts started getting a little bigger, he began to enlarge his shop a little bit," said Clarence Gayle's great-grandson, Currey Gayle of Atlanta.

COURTESY OF CURREY GAYLE

Self-taught engineer Clarence Gayle, who died in 1948, liked to catch fish and make good fishing reels.

"Then he got a contract with Clinton Engineer Works (a contractor with the atomic laboratories in Oak Ridge, Tn.) and wound up producing what he said were about 30,000 parts of 20 different types. He said he was given drawings and asked if he could make the parts. As soon as he finished, he had to return the drawings.

"Of the 20 different parts, there may have been only one that was a true part," Currey Gayle noted. "The other 19 may have just been something to throw off his knowledge of what he was doing."

Not until after the war did Clarence Gayle learn in a letter of appreciation from Gen. H.H. Arnold, commander of the Army Air Forces, that his small shop had been making bomb parts.

Gayle died in 1948 at age 82 and apparently never learned exactly how his parts were used. But his great-grandson said that Gayle had always believed that some of the parts went into the bombsight.

Although the Gayle company's work on the secret Manhattan Project is now an obscure footnote in Frankfort's history, Carlton West, editor of the *Frankfort State Journal*, hopes to one day fill in the missing pages of the company's history - by identifying the specific parts that Gayle made.

"I see it as a journalistic challenge to find the documentation of what Gayle did, what the part was and what it performed," West said.

After Clarence Gayle's death, the company stopped making fishing reels, but still did work for the military. For a time it was the nation's largest manufacturer of military identification plates, commonly known as dog tags.

Footnote: Today some of Gayle's fishing reels sell for thousands of dollars. An exhibit is dedicated to Gayle's memory at the Capital City Museum in Frankfort, Ky.

A Rare Geode

January 7, 1998

H ALLS GAP, Ky. – Squeezing under a dangerous limestone
overhang beside U.S. 27 a few miles south of Stanford in Lincoln County is the next best thing to crawling inside a giant
treasure chest for many geologists, mineralogists and rock collectors.

Despite the growing threat that the earth and limestone overhang will
collapse, the lure of geodes that contain a rare mineral known as millerite
has drawn hundreds of prospectors to Halls Gap since the discovery of
millerite there in 1964. The mineral was named for British mineralogist
William Miller.

"It's really grown to be a world-class locality for millerite, and people
come from all over the world to collect there," said geologist Warren H.
Anderson of the University of Kentucky. "Millerite is hard to collect, but
some nice specimens come out of there. In most mineral books, if you see
pictures of millerite, most of them came from Halls Gap, Kentucky."

Although millerite is known to occur in a few places in Europe and
Canada, and has been found in a few other states, the Lincoln County
site has produced many of the finest specimens found anywhere.

The nickel sulfide deposits appear as delicate crystals that are brassy
yellow to olive metallic. They form a cluster of needle-like strands inside
many geodes. Most are small, about the size of a quarter, but occasionally
a softball-sized specimen is safely dislodged from the ledge.

Anderson, who is the author of "Rocks and Minerals of Kentucky"

106

PHOTO BY BYRON CRAWFORD

(Kentucky Geological Survey), says that professional geologists have yet to unravel the origin of millerite, but he theorizes that the unusual specimens are the product of underground chemical reactions where shale meets siltstone in the Borden geological formation.

"We don't have a clear understanding of why they are localized where they are," he said. "We just have not had time to research it."

Halls Gap, which sits atop a mile-long incline leading up to the Mississippian Plateau, has attracted the attention of scientists from around the world who are interested in its deposits of millerite and other rare minerals.

Honessite, or jamborite, which is green, is an older, more rarely seen, cousin of millerite, and is also found along the road cut at Halls Gap.

"I met a man there once from Israel," recalled Harold Smith, a veteran rock collector who lives a few miles from the gap. "Professors out of some university in Tennessee were digging up there about 1970, and I stopped to see what they were digging. I dug a whole lot after that."

Over the next 15 years Smith estimates he found more than 1,000 millerite geodes, many of which he traded to other collectors on the international market.

Rock collectors Kirtley Settles and Danny Settles, construction contractors in nearby Danville, have two of their millerite specimens on exhibit in the Harvard University Museum and many other specimens in other museums around the country.

"You can go anywhere in the world, and if people have ever heard of millerite, they've heard of Halls Gap," said Kirtley, who is Danny's father.

"I've been in this 30-some years and never sold a mineral, but I've bought a lot and given a lot away. I like to get them out where other people can see them and learn about them."

Although many decent millerite specimens can be bought for $100, exceptional geodes of millerite and honessite often sell

for much more. Kirtley Settles recalls that he once offered another collector $500 for a good millerite geode and was turned down.

The Settleses and other collectors still search the undercut ledge along Halls Gap despite concerns that the site may be unsafe.

"I think it is very dangerous," said Anderson, the UK geologist. "A lot of it is an exposed area where it's probably very highly fractured. I'm afraid someone could get injured, because that thing could just pop right off there."

Footnote: A few years after this story appeared, the highway department filled in the overhang hollowed out by collectors, effectively closing the site.

Ancient Art

August 15, 1999

PETRO>GLYPH (pe'tro glif') n. a rock carving, esp. a prehistoric one. Kentucky has more documented petroglyph sites than any other state east of the Mississippi River, due largely to the work of Dr. Fred Coy of Louisville, a retired orthopedic surgeon and a nationally recognized authority on what is popularly called rock art.

"I happened into this truly by accident," Coy said. "One spring day in 1962, I was walking up the North Fork of Rough River in Breckinridge County, photographing some wildflowers with my friend, Tom Fuller, the best naturalist I've ever known, and he hollered, 'Hey, Doc, come and look at this.'"

There in a small rock shelter above the river Coy and Fuller studied the mysterious grooved markings in the rocks. Some of the carvings resembled bird tracks, one was a human handprint, and a couple were what are commonly called "hominy holes."

PHOTO BY B. CRAWFORD

"I took a picture of them, came back home and tried to look up some information in the library and found nothing written about them," Coy said. "One thing led to another, and here I am today."

Now 75, Coy has spent much of the past 37 years searching out petroglyph sites all over Kentucky, especially along the rim of the Cumberland and Muldraugh escarpments, where such markings are most often found in sandstone shelters and outcroppings.

The Kentucky petroglyphs that he has documented include tracks of various animals, such as bears, minks, elk and rabbits; figures that may depict insects; images of raptorial birds; complex geometric symbols; turtles; human head motifs; hands and feet; and human stick figures, all presumably pecked or scraped into the rock with sharp stone tools.

Besides the petroglyphs, one pictograph (a painted drawing on rock) has been found in Edmonson County. It depicts a human figure and a circular image containing likenesses of a beaver and human forms.

"There are many petroglyphs in the West," Coy explained. "We have found at least 60 petroglyph sites in Kentucky and in all of the eastern United States, there are fewer than 300 rock art sites, but I think that's because many haven't been discovered yet. Very few of these sites in Kentucky have been dated. But I believe a number of them to be as much as 3,000 years old, and perhaps a few, including the pictograph in Edmonson County, no more than a few hundred years old."

Cecil Ison, forest archaeologist for the Daniel Boone National Forest, said Coy has done more than anyone he knows to preserve Kentucky's petroglyphs, and Ison places him among the most knowledgeable sources on petroglyphs in the eastern United States.

Coy says he has found only two petroglyph sites himself, and that all of the others he has documented have been found by such people as hunters, farmers and fellow researchers who have led him to the sites. He credits Larry Meadows, an authority on the Red River Gorge, with locating many of the state's petroglyphs.

Coy is a co-founder and former president of the Eastern States Rock Art Research Association, and is co-author, with Thomas Fuller, Larry Meadows and James Swauger, of the book "Rock Art of Kentucky," published by The University Press of Kentucky.

Their book includes about 175 photographs and illustrations, along with descriptions of Kentucky's petroglyphs. Coy also has thousands of

color slides that he often uses in lectures across the country on petro-glyphs and pictographs.

Coy does not associate any of the Kentucky petroglyphs with, nor does he believe, the legend that a Welsh prince named Madoc visited the region in the 12th century and that his party may have left some of the markings found on rocks here. Coy knows of no archaeologists who accept the Madoc theory.

While many of Kentucky's petroglyphs have remained virtually undisturbed through the ages, one site has been destroyed by vandals, Coy said. Several have been defaced by graffiti, and a number have been destroyed by road builders or by the damming of rivers. In recent years, acid rain has begun to accelerate the erosion of many of the ancient markings.

The meanings of petroglyphs generally remain mysteries.

"I do not try to interpret anything," Coy said. "All I've done is find them and record them. My other mission in life is trying to get people to realize that these are real valuable windows that we have to the past, and that they are disappearing very rapidly."

Elliott County Diamond Mine

September 14, 1981

STEPHENS, Ky. – A U.S. Geological Survey report by geologist J.S. Diller, October 21, 1886, suggested the presence of a valuable diamond field deep in the hills of northeastern Kentucky.

Diller reported: In Elliott County, Kentucky, near Isoms Mill, six miles southwest of Willard, there are two short dikes of peridotite breaking through the horizontal sandstones and shales of carboniferous age."

He added, in substance, that there was every indication that the diamonds to be found in Elliott County were of the same class as those produced in South Africa.

"Peridotite" is loosely defined as a granular rock composed chiefly of an often transparent olive-green magnesium-iron silicate, many of which are used as gemstones.

Willis Everman of Grayson, Kentucky, a veteran surveyor and knowledgeable historian, possesses a copy of another geologist's report which he says has been circulated for many years.

It is dated 1903 and is signed by David Draper, whose address was listed as Johannesburg, Transvaal, (South Africa), where he said he had worked as a geologist for many years.

"So far as is known at present, the only occurrence of Kimberlite

112

outside of the southern portion of Africa is in Elliott County, East Kentucky," the report states.

Kimberlite, also called "blue ground," is found in extinct volcanic craters known as "pipes." The discovery of such mineral-filled craters in 1870 at Kimberley, South Africa, produced one of the largest diamond fields in the world.

The report described the Elliott County field as, "the region lying between Ison and Creeches Creeks, an area in which Kimberlite identical with that contained in the South African pipes has been discovered.

"Every special characteristic of the South African minerals can be duplicated abundantly in the Kentucky Kimberlite," the report said.

At the time the aforementioned reports where written, it is not believed that much diamond exploration had occurred in Elliott County. However, it was not long before work began.

Commencing in 1908 and continuing for about three years, an effort was made to find diamonds.

"At one time it was booming pretty big, mostly men with picks and shovels," commented Isom T. Ison, 78, who has lived near the "diamond field" all his life.

"They came in here and drilled and hit that hard blue stuff," he recalled. "It would wear their bits out it was so hard."

Ison took me up to the "diamond field," warning me to be on the lookout for copperhead snakes, and pointing as we walked to old machines that remained from the days when fortune had been sought here.

It had always been a mysterious place, he said. There was a story handed down in his family about "old Uncle Dave Creech."

He said he had been riding his horse home one night through what they call "the low gap," a dip in the ridge overlooking the field, when he claimed he saw the ground cracked open and a fire shooting up out of it.

It nearly scared Uncle Dave to death. He thought it was the end of time.

"That happened maybe a hundred years before I was born," Ison said. "But I've always heard it, and I believe it's so."

Around the turn of the century, as many as 40 men worked at the mine, including Isom Ison's brother, Ira, who, at age 95, can still recall what it was like.

"They had a big floor there and they'd put that fine dirt on that floor and work 10 hours a day and 10 hours a night. That dirt was just like ashes, nearly. They thought there'd been a big upheaval there."

According to Ira, the principal backers and overseers of the project in 1906 were Austin Q. Millar, a man whose name he recalls as Ned Demins, whose father had a "great interest" in the mine, and John T. Ratliff (or Ratliffe).

Raftliff's name is often mentioned regarding searches in eastern Kentucky for the legendary lost silver mines of John Swift, which will be the subject of another column.

It has been thought that the so-called "diamond field" may have been discovered during a search for one of Swift's mines. Ira Ison said the men who were looking for diamonds in Elliott County wanted to find what they called, "the contact wall."

"They got after me to tell them how far I thought it went before there was any natural mineral like wall. I took 'em up there and old man Millar said, 'We're going to sink a shaft there.'

"They put long logs across that shaft and dug down 42 feet, and some of 'em said, 'Now I don't aim to work down there anymore.'

"They said it stunk, and some said it was getting worse and worse, so they quit."

Millar tried to run a lateral tunnel out at the base of the shaft, according to Ira Ison, but finally abandoned the attempt when no one could be found to dig.

Were any diamonds ever found? "Well now, I don't know," Ira said. "One man around here said they made a report that they found six diamonds. They found some nice garnets – red ones, blue ones and green ones. They claimed they just about paid their expenses up there.

"They'd carry stuff in 10 quart buckets.

ILLUSTRATION BY B. CRAWFORD

They had a big sorting room, and they had two men that followed us at our backs in the sorting room, to see that we emptied our buckets.

"On the Ison Creek side, just below the mouth of Johnson Creek, they sunk a shaft 72 feet deep and found some awful nice garnets."

But soon, Ira said, the ground "commenced shaking and trembling in the shaft, and men got to where they wouldn't work in there either."

It happened that diamonds were found in Arkansas about the same time they were being looked for in Kentucky. And by 1910 the Elliott County field had been abandoned. Willis Everman said that at least twice in the 1950s and 1960s other attempts were made at finding diamonds in Elliott County, apparently with little success.

Were the diamonds never there? Or were they just never found?

Of such questions, prospectors are made.

Swift Silver Legend

May 25, 1983

E VEN before Kentucky was settled there existed the legend of a man named John Swift, whose purported journal tells of silver-mining expeditions into the Kentucky Territory as early as 1760. The tale of Swift's lost silver mines is among the most enduring ever told in Kentucky, and though more than two centuries have passed since Swift is said to have been here, his name is still a household word in the most remote reaches of Eastern Kentucky.

Excerpts of the supposed Swift Journal appeared in Collins' History of Kentucky, Vol. II, published in 1874. One passage reads:

"On the 1st of Sept., 1769, we left between 22,000 and 30,000 dollars and crowns on a large creek, running near a south course. Close to the spot we marked our names (Swift, Jefferson, Munday, and others) on a beech tree with a compass, square and trowel. No great distance from this place we left $15,000 of the same kind, marking three or four trees with marks. Not far from these, we left the prize, near a forked white oak, and about three feet underground, and laid two long stones across it, marking several stones close about it."

It all sounds too good to be true, and many historians believe it is.

Tradition has placed Swift's mine in various places, from Bell County on the south, to Carter County in the north, and even in West Virginia, Virginia, North Carolina and Tennessee.

One early Tennessee historian, Judge John Haywood, said that the earliest settlers in what is now Bell County, Kentucky, found "two old furnaces on Clear Creek that exhibited very ancient appearances," and showed no evidence of having been used for iron smelting. Similar furnaces, he said, were found on the South Fork of the Cumberland River.

Haywood claimed that a man named Swift passed through Bean's Station in Tennessee in 1790, on his way to the furnaces, and that he carried with him a journal of former transactions by which it appeared that he and his party had operated the furnaces on Clear Creek from 1761 through 1763, and later, in 1767, had a furnace near the Red Bird fork of the Kentucky River.

Haywood wrote that Swift and his associates made silver in "large quantities" at this location, adding, "they got the ore from a cave about three miles from the place where his furnace stood."

The latter portions of Swift's purported journal spell out in some detail the location of the mines.

"The richest ore is to be found in Latitude 37 degrees, 56 minutes north (some versions read 57 minutes). The ore vein of little value is in Latitude of 38 degrees, 2 minutes north. By astronomical observations and calculations we found both veins to be just a little west of the longitude of 83 degrees."

The area described is roughly five square miles, near the point where Elliott, Lawrence and Morgan Counties meet.

Joe Nickell, an instructor of technical writing at the University of Kentucky, has researched the Swift legend and does not believe there ever was such a person who mined silver in Kentucky.

Although there was a Jonathan Swift who lived in Alexandria, Virginia, during the late 1700s, Nickell says, there is no evidence that he ever came to Kentucky or engaged in mining ventures.

Nickell theorizes that the "Swift journal" may have been written by early Kentucky historian John Filson as an allegory related to Free Masonry, which later played a significant role in numerous land schemes.

Michael Paul Henson of Jeffersonville, Indiana, a widely read writer on the Swift Mines and other lost treasures, is convinced that the story is real.

Footnote: Geologists generally scoff at legends that have been passed down about gems and precious metals in Kentucky, yet the stories survive. In the Twelfth Biennial Report of the Bureau of Agriculture, Labor and Statistics of *the state of Kentucky in 1897, the report on Hardin County stated: "Recently there has been discovered at Summit, two gold mines which are now being worked and assay from $34 to $54 to the ton of ore." I visited the purported site a few years ago and found only some scattered rocks.*

Mandy Tree

October 30, 1996

MADISONVILLE, Ky. – This was not a typical haunting, Ron Elliott assured me. It was a very special story with some strange twists.

So strange that even through the mist of well over half a century, the story of Madisonville's "Mandy Tree" is one of Kentucky's classic ghost tales.

Elliott, whose grandparents, H.V. and Madeline C. Taylor, once owned property where the tree stood, knows a few details of the story that many outsiders have never heard.

In the 1920s, or earlier, a woman named Amanda Taylor Holloman died mysteriously in her Madisonville home while her husband was away at work. Fragments of old news accounts say that Holloman's grown stepson had been in the home the morning it happened, and that her two younger children returned from getting water at a nearby spring to find her lifeless, nude body wrapped in a quilt.

The stories claim that she was later found to have been shot under the right arm. There were reports that the stepson was seen running from the home not long before she was discovered and that he arrived late that morning at the coal mine where he worked. But he reportedly told police he had left the house right after his father left for work, and he wasn't charged.

Although Amanda Holloman's death was officially listed as a suicide,

119

her family and friends always thought she had been murdered.

Her husband gave up the children and finally left town, and memories of Amanda eventually faded.

In time the property where she had died - including a white oak tree that she had loved and nurtured in the back yard - passed into the hands of Elliott's grandparents, the Taylors, who were African Methodist Episcopal ministers.

Elliott's grandmother told family members that she and her husband feared at one point that they could not make the mortgage payments and might lose the property. But she said that she began praying that a way would be provided to save the place.

That was when someone noticed that Amanda's favorite tree, the white oak in the yard, had grown into a silhouette of her looking up into the heavens. Those who knew Amanda agreed that her facial features, hairstyle, and even her high collar could be seen in the shape of the tree's foliage.

Eventually thousands of sightseers flocked to the Taylor home on West Broadway to see the tree – especially on nights when the moon was behind it. Ron Elliott, a professional photographer, says that he has seen a photograph of the Mandy Tree on a page from Life magazine that his stepmother has hanging on her wall in Detroit.

"My grandmother

Madisonville's "Mandy Tree" as pictured in the 1930s.

would sell refreshments and things like that, and my grandfather sold picture postcards of the tree," Elliott said. "They didn't get rich off of it or anything, but they made enough to keep the land."

Details are now dim as to how many years the tree's foliage held Amanda Holloman's silhouette, but Elliott's grandmother told the family that as soon as the mortgage was paid off, the tree began to lose its ghostly shape.

Lightning destroyed the tree soon after Elliott's grandmother died, years ago.

PHOTO BY BYRON CRAWFORD

Ron Elliott's grandparents once owned the ghostly "Mandy Tree."

First-Hand Experience

February 7, 1999

ARTHUR, Tenn. – When Wilson Collins heard the news that the first hand transplant in the United States had been performed in Louisville Jan. 24, his memories carried him back to his own similar medical first, eighteen years earlier.

In 1981, Collins, a former resident of Eastern Kentucky, became the first person in the world to have the hand from one arm transplanted to the opposite arm after an accident at a coal company. His surgery also was performed in Louisville, by one of the surgeons who served on last month's hand transplant team, Dr. Joseph Kutz.

"God gave Dr. Kutz the gift of knowledge to do it, and gave me the strength to learn to use it," Collins said last week. "I've learned to eat with the hand, write, shave, bathe and dress myself, and drive anywhere I want to. I do all the grocery shopping."

On an icy night in December 1981, Collins was fueling a 50-ton truck loaded with rock at a Lost Mountain Mining Co. site in Perry County, Ky., when the truck lurched backward, trapping him between it and another truck. The accident instantly severed his right hand and knocked him to the ground, the truck running over his other arm and hand, cutting his throat and breaking both jaws.

"When I got on my back and raised my right arm up, all I could see was that there wasn't no hand there. My hand was up in the back of that truck somewhere," Collins recalled. "I just said, 'God have mercy upon my family.'"

Collins, then 38 and a resident of Perry County, was still conscious when he was taken to the Appalachian Regional Hospital in Hazard, then flown to Louisville's Jewish Hospital, also the site of last month's hand transplant.

"We tried first of all to save his right arm, and realized we couldn't," Kutz recalled. "Then the left hand we knew was severely crushed, and we realized we couldn't save that. Then we said: 'Well, he's got a good hand and good tendons. Why don't we try to do something with the other side?' So we moved him over, hooked up the bone, then hooked up the artery - and it flowed well, so we went ahead and repaired the rest of the structure."

Collins, who had been right-handed, awoke to find that his right arm had been amputated at the shoulder and that his severed right hand had been attached to his left arm about thre inches above the wrist. When he was finally able to examine the hand, palm up, his thumb was where his little finger should have been. He was looking at the palm of his right hand on the end of his left arm.

"We hooked up the major nerves in the same line, and the tendons, so that when he pulls his thumb ... the orientation is the same, so he knows it's his thumb or his little finger. Unfortunately, his hand is in a fixed position. He cannot put his hand flat down or turn it up," Kutz said. "I've tried to talk to him about letting us move his thumb to the opposite side, but he says, no, that it's working fine the way it is. His handwriting is plainer than mine."

Collins cannot close his fingers more than about halfway, and instead of being rotated at the wrist, the hand can only be rotated by moving the entire arm. However, Collins has improvised methods of lighting

PHOTO BY BYRON CRAWFORD

123

cigarettes, starting his car, fastening his belt and performing many other daily routines. He usually carries change in his shirt pockets for the convenience of store clerks.

Today, Collins and his wife, Linda, live just across the Tennessee line from Middlesboro, Ky. Both are disabled. Collins credits his strong faith, his wife and their two children, Jimmy and Haley, with helping him through the most difficult years of rehabilitation, when he was practically helpless.

Although he got a settlement from the mining company after his accident, it was not enough to send his children to college - one of his biggest regrets - or to keep him from losing a small parcel of land on which he and his wife had planned to retire, he said.

Collins hopes that some day he can meet recent hand-transplant recipient Matthew Scott of New Jersey and offer a few words of encouragement.

"I'd just like to have a conversation with him over a cup of coffee," Collins said. "Sometimes that's all it takes."

Haunted Radio Station

October 29, 1995

C YNTHIANA, Ky. – Halloween is getting to be pretty much a year-round affair at radio station WCYN-AM/FM in Cynthiana. Many employees of the station claim the place is haunted. Ghost tales have persisted for years about the historic log building, circa 1790s, which served as Harrison County's first courthouse and in which statesman Henry Clay practiced law in 1817. Later, Cynthiana's first newspaper was published in the building, and at the turn of the century, it housed a photographic studio. The radio station moved into the building on the town square in 1973.

Chris Winkle, the program director and morning on-air personality, said that soon after he came to the station in 1991, he often noticed shadows moving on the windows between studios as he signed the station on the air in the predawn hours, alone in the building.

"I knew there really shouldn't be shadows there," he said, "but I got to where it didn't bother me. Then one morning I was sitting there ... and something actually turned the corner and went down the stairs, and that put the fear in me."

Winkle described the form, which he has seen twice, as that of a man of medium build with gray hair.

He last saw the figure early one morning in February of this year. Winkle said he came down the back stairs to the kitchen, opened the refrigerator, and, as he turned, noticed the form of the man disappearing

125

PHOTO BY BYRON CRAWFORD

Anne Anderson

around the corner into the darkened hallway at the bottom of the stairs.

"This time it apparently had been following me … and from what I remember, when I looked, I saw a left shoulder facing me, with him going in the opposite direction, and then I saw the back. I've never seen his face, but he appears to be the same guy, with gray hair, and wearing maybe a brown pullover sweater."

Anne Anderson, the station's owner and general manager, says that she has yet to see or hear anything supernatural at the station. But she says that one former female employee is convinced that the ghostly figure she saw in the control room early one morning was that of Anderson's late husband, Reed, an electronics engineer who co-founded the station with his wife in 1956 and died several years ago.

"I don't know whether she'd talk about it or not, but she worked here for 22 years," Anderson said. "She was up at the control board and she said she felt like something was at her back. She sort of turned around, and she said that there was my husband – just as solid as we are – in the control room behind her. For a split second, she said, she didn't even think that it was not him, until she turned her face back to the board and thought, 'That can't be Reed,' and she turned back around and he was gone."

Staff members say that heavy doors – even when left locked – are often heard slamming loudly and repeatedly at the station at all hours. A commode upstairs often flushes by itself, and a motion-detecting alarm in the station frequently goes off without explanation. Footsteps and clanging metal are often heard, and the police have even been called to search for intruders.

Lee Hamovitz, a former news director at the station, said he left late one night without locking the place after he went into the kitchen for a glass of water and the lid on a box of doughnuts on the table flapped up and down several times.

"I was terrified," Hamovitz recalled. "I'm a skeptical person, but I can figure no natural explanation for this, because it went up and down a good half-dozen times, quickly, like a playing card in a bicycle spoke."

George Slade, 79, a local historian, had his own ghost experience at the log house when he was 10. One stormy afternoon he crawled through a hole in the wall at the rear of the building near an old stairwell to take shelter from the rain.

"I heard a squeak, like someone coming down those steps," Slade remembered. "Everything seemed to get real warm and still, but it was still pouring rain. Then I heard this voice say, 'Mac,' and I heard another voice say, 'Elizabeth,' kind of in a whisper. I was standing back against the wall with water dripping down on my head. I kind of moved away and got into some cobwebs, and I heard this voice again say, 'Mac,' and 'Elizabeth,' and I took off in the rain – and didn't tell anybody for years."

Not until many years later did Slade learn that one of the building's early owners was a man named McPheeters. His wife's name was Elizabeth.

Footnote: The radio station no longer makes its home in the old log building.

Famous UFO Footnote?

October 9, 1994

APT. Thomas Mantell Jr. must have thought it strange – a UFO report from Fort Knox on that cold Jan. 7 afternoon in 1948 when the control tower at the Army post's Godman Field radioed his pursuit plane to check out a gleaming unidentified flying object sighted in the direction of Bowling Green.

When the call came, Mantell, 25, was leading a flight of three propeller-driven Kentucky Air National Guard P-51s back from a routine training mission to Atlanta. He and his fellow pilots responded, but the two other planes, having no oxygen, abandoned the chase. Mantell continued through the broken clouds. He radioed the tower: "I'm closing in now to take a good look. It's directly ahead of me and moving at about half my speed. The thing looks metallic, and it's tremendous in size."

Not long afterward, radio contact was lost, and about 35 minutes later Mantell's P-51 exploded in the air as it was diving toward earth, not far from Franklin in Simpson County.

The crash became one of the country's most famous UFO incidents – chronicled by many news reports as the first UFO fatality in the world. Air Force investigators later theorized that the object Mantell described was either the planet Venus, which was extremely bright at that time of year, or a weather balloon.

Now, there may be new light on the mystery.

Last Thursday, from his home in Socorro, N.M., retired balloon scientist Charles Moore, former engineer in charge of the Navy's Project Skyhook, said he is all but certain that Mantell was chasing a balloon that he helped launch.

Moore, 74, a professor emeritus of atmospheric physics at the New Mexico Institute of Mining and Technology, said that on Jan. 6, 1948, at Camp Ripley, Minn., he helped prepare, launch and track a Navy Skyhook balloon that, when fully inflated, was 105 feet tall and nearly 73 feet in diameter.

He said the helium-filled balloon lifted 90,000 feet into the frigid sky, and then flew to the southeast over Illinois, Kentucky, Tennessee, and South Carolina before it finally blew out to sea and vanished without ever releasing a parachute that held its payload of scientific information.

"It was a cosmic-ray balloon that carried a cloud chamber designed to test high-energy particles that come in from outside our atmosphere," Moore said. "It was not metallic. It was polyethylene, like a garment-cleaning bag, about one one-thousandth of an inch thick. But if you were at the right angle relative to the sun, it could have appeared metallic. Otto Winnzen (the project chief) essentially tracked the balloon by

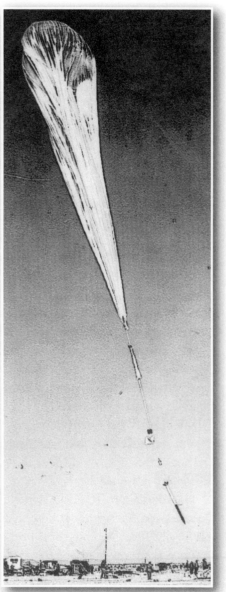

PHOTO COURTESY CHARLES B. MOORE

The helium-filled Navy Skyhook weather balloon glistened in the sun as it was launched in January of 1948 at Camp Ripley, Minn. The balloon was 105 feet tall.

129

the reports of an unidentified object. He was quite sure that the sighting over Godman Field, Ky., was the balloon.

"The Navy was not at all interested in having the idea put out at the time that the flight that caused Captain Mantell's death was a result of one of their experiments, but we strongly believed it was so. My memory is that I was cautioned by local Navy officers involved with the project not to say anything about it," Moore said. "I deeply regret that someone got killed … and I have a deep feeling against cover-ups. I'd like to see my history correct."

Captain Mantell

A spokesman for the Office of Naval Research in Washington said he could neither support nor deny Moore's statements. However, he confirmed that Skyhook balloons, which were classified "confidential," were being used for atmospheric testing by the Navy during 1948 in central Minnesota.

Mantell's wife, Margaret, now remarried and still living in Louisville, was not allowed to see the wreckage of her husband's plane. She said she was told that pieces of it were sent to Dayton, Ohio, for investigation, and that her husband had passed out from oxygen starvation before the crash. Mantell, who had been among the first fliers to cross the Cherbourg Peninsula on D-Day and was awarded the Distinguished Flying Cross for heroism during World War II, was buried at Zachary Taylor National Cemetery in Louisville.

His oldest son, Thomas Mantell III of Louisville, was not aware of Moore's account of the skyhook balloon but said he had heard mention of the skyhook theory in some of the many stories on the incident.

He is skeptical, however, that a balloon could have been flying half the speed of a P-51, as his father's radio message indicated.

"The cover-up is the big thing," Mantell said. "They were very vague with my mom…. She, like me, believed that he was too good a pilot to have gone too high and blacked out from lack of oxygen. He'd flown too many missions without oxygen, and he knew his capabilities. I would really like to know the real cause of the crash. That's what befuddles me more than anything."

P-47 Lost and Found

December 21, 1903

WORLD War II fighter pilot John Treitz of Louisville is one of those veterans who rarely discusses his military service. That might be why it took one of his friends a while to spread the news about pieces of Treitz's old P-47 Thunderbolt having been rescued from a watery grave in Europe and finding their way back to Treitz more that 50 years after the war.

"Unbelievable" was the only word Treitz could find to describe the news two years ago that researchers in Belgium had found the mangled wreckage and were searching for the plane's name.

"Jeannie" was the name Treitz had painted on the P-47, in the style of his wife Jeannie's signature.

Treitz, now 83, joined the Army Air Corps in March 1942. He married his sweetheart, Jeannie Barnhill of Louisville, on his way to the East Coast from flight training in Arizona the following November. Soon he was flying combat missions over France and Belgium with the 353rd Fighter Group, with which he is reputed to have been the first U.S. pilot to dive-bomb in Europe.

During 200 hours of combat duty in which half of the 24 pilots in his 351st squadron were killed, Treitz earned two Distinguished Flying Crosses and four Air Medals.

Treitz and the winged "Jeannie" shared many close calls and adventures in the skies over Europe. One day German flak struck his plane and his engine died about 100 miles deep in German territory.

In the split second that his engine went silent and the plane began free-falling from 35,000 feet, his whole life, all 22 years of it, really did pass through his mind, Treitz said. Gasoline was running into the plane's floorboard as he frantically switched gas tanks and managed to restart the sputtering engine. He headed for the English Channel, beyond which lay his airfield. The plane ran out of gas just as it touched down. It was later discovered that a gas line had been partially severed by flak.

PHOTO FROM FAMILY ARCHIVES

Like so many of his fellow veterans, Treitz has never understood how he survived the war when a number of his friends were shot down around him, and thousands upon thousands of other good airmen, soldiers, sailors and Marines never made it home.

When his combat duty ended and he began training new pilots in northern England in the spring of 1944, Treitz lost track of his old fighter plane.

Only two years ago, after making the acquaintance of the plane's second pilot during a chance meeting at an Army reunion, did he learn that "Jeannie" had been part of the D-Day invasion of Normandy and had been shot down about three months later over Belgium. William Barlow, now 79 and living in Bainbridge Island, Washington, bailed out and survived, but lost both legs below the knees after wandering lost in a forest behind enemy lines for days.

During the mid-1980s, a researcher found wreckage of the plane submerged in a bog and recovered a few machine gun serial numbers, which he traced though Washington and eventually to the pilots. He tracked down Treitz to ask the name of the plane and to see if there were any pictures of the aircraft and photos of the woman for whom it was named, for placement in a museum exhibit near Vender, Belgium.

Treitz, a retired highway contractor who is now a developer, later was sent a part of the feeding and ejection mechanisms for the plane's machine gun as keepsakes. The pieces, along with pictures of the P-47 and photos of his daughter, also named Jeannie, hang on the wall of his home in eastern Louisville; the home he shares with the Jeannie, whose name he wrote on the side of a fighter plane an ocean away, 60 years ago.

Bath County Badlands

March 18, 1994

O
WINGSVILLE, Ky. – It is almost as if a giant hand had picked up several acres of South Dakota's Badlands and dropped them in the middle of Bath County.

The Knob Licks, as they are known locally, have been a geological curiosity as far back as anyone remembers. Nearly any older native of the county can recall when picnicking at the knobs was an annual rite of spring. Many old photograph albums in the county show faded pictures of someone in the family posing atop one of the pale, plantless ridges of clay and shale that crisscross the knobs between gullies 30 to 40 feet deep. Ben Staton, 64, whose father once owned the knobs, remembers playing on the steep, narrow ridges when he was a boy.

"We used to ride ponies across these knobs and would fall off, but in that clay dirt it wouldn't hurt," he said.

"I could be mistaken, but in my young days, one Easter Sunday, I believe they claimed there was cars there from 40 of the 48 states. They'd park and go to the Knob Licks on Easter Sunday every year. I mean big crowds. That was one of the main attractions."

Scrub cedars and pines rim the 10- to 15-acre basin where the knobs are located, but the ridges themselves are devoid of vegetation. Staton remembers that years ago, youngsters gave the ridges such names as Devil's Backbone, Camel Back and Main Ridge. The site was once a popular spot for school field trips, and Staton says there was even some talk once of building a commercial lodge there, but the building never materialized.

Over the years the knobs have virtually been forgotten, but their strange topography has changed very little. They are on private property some three miles south of the Licking River, not more than a mile from where a 19th-century iron-smelting furnace was located. After the Civil War and up until 1914, strip-mining of iron ore was one of Bath County's major industries. But Staton says he is certain that the mysterious knobs were not part of the iron mines. They bear no resemblance to the abandoned mine sites, he said, and old-timers who remembered the mining op-

Ben Staton, left, and his son, Woody Staton, looked over the weathered clay formations at Knob Licks in Bath County.

erations of long ago always said that no ore was ever taken from the Knob Licks.

Perhaps the knobs were placed there by Mother Nature as a place for shadows to play with the sun, or for ponies and youngsters to play cowboys and Indians, or for all those thousands who took Easter picnics there long ago and made pictures of each other in Bath County's very own badlands.

"At one time," Staton said, "nobody had ever seen anything like them."

Mystery Canal

November 11, 1994

C LINTON, Ky. – One of Hickman County's most mysterious landmarks, and perhaps one of its most historic, is a four-and-a-half-mile-long canal that connects Bayou de Chien and Obion Creek – the county's two largest Mississippi River tributaries.

Some people call the waterway Lake Slough, Dry Lake or Indian Canal. But most locals just call it Dug Ditch. Any one of the names is enough to start an argument among archaeologists, geologists and historians about the origin of the deep channel that now is guarded by towering cypress, some of which are more than four feet in diameter. Local legend has it that the canal, which cuts through the lowlands at a depth of some 15 feet and a width of more than 80 feet in places, was dug by prehistoric mound builders who lived along the high bluff overlooking the nearby Mississippi River. The canal runs in nearly a straight line north and south over its greater length, while most other streams in the area meander east and west. Near its northern end, the canal turns west at almost a right angle and joins the current of Obion Creek. Water still flows in the channel during wet months.

Archaeologists have found the remains of villages, burial grounds and earthen mounds that were prehistoric temple sites near the point where Dug Ditch enters Bayou de Chien. These findings, coupled with the straightness and dimensions of the long canal, have furthered speculation that the waterway was man-made.

Mary Sue Whayne, a local historian, says many researchers think the canal may have been built as an express route for travel between two large prehistoric villages that have been discovered near each end of the channel.

"The story has been passed down from generation to generation, and people here say that the ditch pretty much looks the same as it did as far back as anyone can remember," Whayne said. "Last spring I sent in to the Kentucky Historical Society and asked them if we could get a historical marker for it."

In her book "Lickskillet and Other Tales of Hickman County," historian Virginia Jewell notes that some researchers have suggested that mound-builders may have "washed out" the deep ditch by directing overflow from Bayou de Chien and Obion Creek to build the shortcut from one stream to the other.

"Or perhaps the channel was patiently dug by hand and the dirt carried out by the basketful," Jewell wrote. "Since greater and more awesome engineering feats of ancient origin exist throughout the world, one would not wish to rule out such a possibility without further study.... Sections of (the ditch) a half mile in length are so straight that a spectator might fancy that it had been laid out by an engineer and dug with a bulldozer."

The late Willard R. Jillson, a prominent Kentucky geologist and historian, offered a contrasting opinion 40 years ago.

"This channel is of natural origin and is not in any way the work of man, the Indian and the mound-builder included, as I see it," Jillson responded. "There is no mystery about it, and no one should be left to believe that such is the case. Running water did this job in this area ... Man – early, late or present – had no part in it," he concluded.

"We don't believe that," said Mary Sue Whayne.

White Hummingbird

September 3, 2003

R AYMOND Young was repairing a hummingbird feeder outside his kitchen window in early August when a snow-white hummingbird landed on the feeder next to his hand.

"I couldn't believe it," Young said. "His wing would hit my hand every once in a while."

Wilma Young said her husband kept yelling for her to come to the window to witness the sight, but she didn't hear him, so he began tapping on the glass.

"The bird sat there through all of that and was still there when I came in," she said. "I didn't think about taking a picture. I just stood and jumped up and down."

Since then she has used nearly a whole roll of film taking pictures of "Snowflake," who visits the two feeders on the Young's deck several times each day and chases away other hummingbirds.

"The white hummer at the Youngs is worthy of all the excitement," said Bill Hilton Jr., executive director of the Hilton Pond Center for Piedmont Natural History in York, South Carolina. It is one of slightly more than 100 documented sightings of white hummingbirds reported in the nation since 1865.

"A woman in Oklahoma has been compiling all the sightings from literature and elsewhere, and that's how many we have records for," Hilton explained. "Obviously, there have been other birds out and about, but people didn't know where to report them."

Hilton guessed that "Snowflake" is probably a female ruby throated hummingbird and is not a true albino. The bird's dark, instead of pinkish, eyes, beak and feet suggest it is a genetic anomaly that occasionally produces a beige or spotted bird, and sometimes birds with white heads or individual white feathers.

Curiously, Hilton said, there has never been a recorded case of a white hummingbird returning in a later year.

Raymond and Wilma Young, and "Snowflake"

Perhaps it is because white birds are more susceptible to predators. But there is also a belief among some scientists that the structural pigment of white feathered hummingbirds may be more brittle than that of other birds, and that their feathers may simply wear out sooner.

Brainard Palmer-Ball, terrestrial zoologist for the Kentucky Nature Preserves Commission, said he gets a report of a white or pale-colored hummingbird in Kentucky about two out of every three years.

Footnote: The Youngs were hopeful that the white hummingbird might set a record by returning for a second summer to their feeder in Henry County, but they never saw her again after the summer of 2003.

Horsehair Snakes

March 4, 1992

SOME columnists hypothesize about global warming, the Soviet metamorphosis, political undercurrents and overdrafts.

I much prefer writing about buttercups and spring peepers, fresh honeysuckle, doodle-bugs and today's subject – horsehair snakes. Claude Rodgers phoned a few days ago to say that he is 80 years old; that he grew up on a 400-acre farm on what now is Fort Knox Army Reservation property in Bullitt County; and that he remembers seeing things called "horsehair snakes" when he was a boy.

He wanted to know if I'd ever seen one, and how it looked, and if I knew what horsehair snakes really were.

Rodgers said he had never believed the story that the snakes were horsehairs that had somehow turned into snakes, but he knew he'd seen them, and indeed they did resemble a horsehair that had come to life. He said he had talked with several people who'd heard of them, but none who had actually seen one.

I told him that I could recall having seen only one in my life, when I was a boy of about 10. It was no more than 8 to 10 inches long, a dark brown or gray wispy thing, resembling a long strand of hair from a horse's mane or tail, slithering across the water with the motion of a snake. I found it in a wet weather spring where I often went to chase tadpoles and water bugs.

Rodgers said he could remember once seeing three or four horsehair

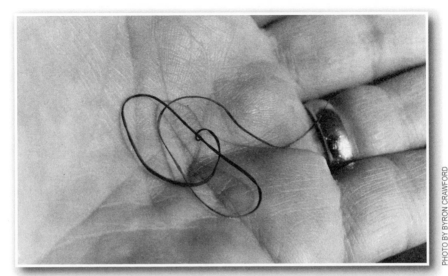

The horsehair snake is really a gordian worm and has nothing to do with horses.

snakes at one time, floating down Salt River. The ones he saw appeared to be 15 to 20 inches long, he said. He has not seen one since he was about 14.

University of Louisville biologists Charles Covell and Fred Whittaker say that they usually get a few reports every year of horsehair snakes – that they say are really worms. The scientific name is nematomorpha.

As larvae, they live in the body cavities of grasshoppers, crickets, beetles, spiders and hundreds of other insects.

As adults, they live freely in wet environments, along streams and in other moist places, and may sometimes reach lengths of 25 to 30 inches. The term "horsehair" is a misnomer, Whittaker says, because other than resembling horsehair, the worm has no connection with horses.

A more proper common name for the creature is the gordian worm, which derives from a knotted rope that confounded Alexander the Great in the ancient city of Gordium.

"Because these worms tie themselves in terribly complex knots, they're called gordian worms," Whittaker explained.

A few years ago, a man found two of the worms knotted up, still alive, in a shower head at his home in north-central Kentucky, Whittaker said.

The worms are harmless. They have a tiny mouth, but it is not used in the adult stage. Rather, the worms absorb their food through the walls of their bodies. Even their larvae, if ingested by a human, would pass harmlessly through the body.

"People used to find them a lot in their dogs' watering dishes, or they'd find them in watering troughs, where an insect had crawled in or fallen in, and the worm had emerged after detecting water," Whittaker explained.

Occasionally, adult worms spend the winter in the soil and emerge in the spring. Although they produce vast numbers of eggs, most people spend a lifetime without ever seeing a horsehair snake.

Claude Rodgers, and a north-central Kentucky man who now checks his shower head often, were the exceptions.

A Bird In The Hand

August 11, 2006

I T happened as quietly as the whisper of hummingbird wings on the soft breath of summer. There were no "Breaking News" alerts on the TV networks, no news helicopters dispatched to the scene, no headlines in the morning papers.

Only a smile on the face of 62-year-old Russell Thompson who, after seven years of feeding and photographing hummingbirds, watched in amazement and delight as a ruby-throat hovered just above his hand and sipped nectar from his palm.

He captured the moment with his digital camera. Otherwise, there would have been no proof of this magnificent event.

Thompson, a retired Jefferson County computer technology teacher and basketball coach in middle and high schools, became fascinated with hummingbirds while visiting relatives in southeastern Kentucky in 1999.

"I came right back home and put up some feeders," he said. "Then I bought a digital camera and the first nature photos I really ever took were of hummingbirds."

Thompson might just as easily have chosen to photograph butterflies or flowers, but there was something in the nature of hummingbirds that drew him closer: How could they find their way from his flower garden near Iroquois Park in Louisville to some tropical forest in Central America for the winter, then return the following spring to the same feeders in his back yard, or even to a favorite flower garden in Canada?

143

He marveled at their ability to fly forward, backwards, straight up and straight down, maneuvering to avoid or attack other hummingbirds in their territorial air battles over his back yard.

Once, when a hummingbird slammed headlong into the sliding glass door on his deck and knocked itself out, he gently cradled it in his hands and stroked it with his fingers for several minutes, until it regained its senses and flew away.

His close encounters with the bird in the hand have occurred in a community flower garden at Riverside, the Farnsley-Mormen Landing, in southwestern Jefferson County, where Thompson maintains feeders and flowers that attract hummingbirds.

"It was hard to believe until I saw it happen, but I've seen it twice now," said Pat O'Leary, the Farnsley-Mormen gardener. "That hummingbird comes right to his hand."

Thompson's friendship with the hummingbird began several weeks ago as he was changing feeders and the impatient male ruby-throat perched on the feeder that he was holding. Later, the bird fed on wildflowers that Thompson brought from home. Then it began perching on Thompson's thumb and drinking from the feeder, and finally hovering just above his hand to feed on nectar from his palm.

"The first thing I noticed was the air from his wings, blowing on my hand, and then when he started eating, his tongue actually touched my hand," Thompson said. "Normally, his feet are within one-tenth of an inch of my hand. My next goal is to have him perch on my thumb and eat from my hand."

Footnote: Incredibly, the ruby-throated hummingbird that sipped nectar from Thompson's hand in the fall returned the following spring on April 30th and began eating from his hand again. "He's the same one," Thompson said, "because it would have taken a lot longer to train a new one."

Pete

November 23, 2007

G EORGETOWN, Ky. – Pete the talking crow lived only about three years in Georgetown, from 1829 to 1832. But during his short life, he left a mark on the city's history that has earned him a permanent exhibit in the Georgetown-Scott County Museum nearly two centuries later.

The story goes that Pete was the property of Dave Adams, who operated a hat shop in town and regularly attended horse races at a track on the edge of Georgetown. Some race starters in those days yelled "Go!" to send off the horses, and it's widely recorded that, without any prompting, one day Pete yelled "Go!" in the excitement of the start. He was rewarded with heavy applause.

B.O. Gaines' "History of Scott County, Kentucky, Vol. II," states that soon after the crow discovered that he could yell "Go!" he began to say it often around the horses.

"Although Pete was able to give the word with all the distinction and vim of a regular starter, he sometimes lacked judgment," Gaines wrote. "He sent them many bad starts. He is quoted as the origin of the use of the bell, his words being mistaken for those of the starter and the horses sent away when the starter had no intention of doing so."

There is an account of Pete's having frightened a drunken wagon driver so badly by alighting on the wagon and yelling, "Bill, oh Bill, oh Bill!"—that the driver rolled off into the mud and was nearly run over by his own wagon.

Townspeople declared that Pete often greeted them with "Good morning," followed by "A cold, frosty morning!" as they passed the hat shop.

One man said the crow said, "They haven't got as much as I could eat" to a passer-by on the way to the market with a basket on his arm.

Pete was said to be able to mimic the voices of some of the locals, and he seemed to know when to use certain phrases. He may have learned a number of profanities from fishermen whose minnows he often stole from their buckets.

Gen. Thomas C. Flournoy wrote that the darkest shade on Pete's character was a tendency for profane swearing when he was upset. After pulling feathers out of a woman's hat

An animatronic replica of Pete at the Georgetown–Scott County Museum

PHOTO BY BYRON CRAWFORD

and being put out of her house, he is said to have told her, "Curse your soul, I'll tell George Sawyer." George worked at the hat shop.

In 1832 Pete was shot by a boy who was visiting Georgetown and presumed him to be an ordinary crow. Pete was buried in a little coffin in a now-unmarked grave on the grounds of Georgetown College, with a sorrowful crowd in attendance as the college bell tolled.

Today, an animatronic, talking replica of Pete greets visitors to the museum, not in his native tongue but in Japanese. Museum director John Toncray explained that in 2000, with a grant from Toyota Motor Manufacturing, Kentucky, Inc., the Pete replica was programmed in Japanese and flown to Japan for a long visit to Georgetown's sister city, Taharo-Cho. Toncray and museum program coordinator Andrew Green now use Pete as a teaching tool for children who have made him one of the musem's most popular exhibits.

Discussion has beeen given to placement of a monument to Pete the talking crow, but no official action has been taken.

Fox Squirrel Attack

June 15, 2005

"**B**IZARRE." That's the word Kenzie Ison used to describe the behavior of a large male fox squirrel that attacked and bit his 10-year-old son, Kaleb, and later attacked and bit him, and reportedly either jumped on or bit several other people in the Owens Branch area of Perry County over the past three weeks.

"My son said he was going up the road on his bike and saw the squirrel sitting in the tree, and stopped and said, 'Hello, little squirrelly,'" Ison said. "At which time it jumped off the tree and took after him. He tried to ride away from it, and it got up on his bicycle a couple of times, then got up on his leg, and he had short pants on, and it sliced his leg above his right ankle, across the back side.

Dr. J. Dustin Chaney, the attending emergency room physician at Appalachian Regional Hospital in Hazard where the boy was treated, said he had never encountered such an incident involving a squirrel and was not able to find any such reference in a medical literature review.

"There were two puncture marks where the squirrel had bitten him, and there was probably about a three-inch laceration across the Achilles tendon where the squirrel had gotten hold of him, and there were a lot of other scratches on his leg," Chaney said.

Diane Sparkman, a Perry County school bus driver who lives near where Kaleb was attacked, said she and her mother had stopped their car to chat with Kaleb's friend, 11-year old Logan Sexton, who was fishing

147

in a stream nearby. She said they heard Kaleb screaming and looked up to see the squirrel chasing him as he rode toward their car.

"It chased me 50 or 60 yards and jumped up on my tire a few times, and whenever I got off I kicked it, and it bit me," Kaleb said. "They told me to get in the car, I watched it, and it was attacking my bike."

Melissa Sheppherd, a nurse who lives nearby, administered first-aid to Kaleb's wounds.

"The state veterinarian's office gave us some good news, that they've never had a case of rabies involving a squirrel, which was my worry," said Kenzie Ison, an herb exporter.

In the meantime, several residents began telling of their run-ins with apparently the same squirrel. David Patterson said he was washing his truck one day when the squirrel ran up his leg and he knocked it off. He was not bitten.

Dr. Mike Auslander, state public health veterinarian, said the squirrel might have been someone's pet at one time, or "there are lots of different diseases that cause brain infections or behavior changes."

After the squirrel chased his son and a friend the second time a few days ago and bit his son on the boot, Ison said he took out his shotgun.

"I walked all the way up past where it happened before, and turned around and started walking back down, and I stepped over into the edge of a lady's yard and was looking up in the trees, and the next thing I know it hits me right in the middle of the back," Ison said.

The animal fell onto Ison's right leg and bit his inner thigh near the groin before he was able to knock it to the ground and kick it into the yard.

"Then it comes back at me, and I don't have time to shoot, so I golf club it with my shotgun barrel," he said. "It rolls out through the grass and gets up and shakes that off and comes at me again, and I golf club it again. It did that three times."

Finally, Ison was able to get a shot off as the squirrel retreated, and he eventually killed the animal, which will be examined by state health officials.

"It sounds like this squirrel has been fed by people, but that's still a pretty big step for a squirrel to be habituated by people and get violent," said biologist John Morgan of the Kentucky Department of Fish and Wildlife Resources. "It is probably unlikely that it is rabies, but it would seem wise to test it."

Footnote: Tests on the squirrel revealed that it did not have rabies. The cause of its behavior is still unknown. But Ison believes someone may have kept the animal as a pet and turned it loose when it became unmanageable.

Continental Palomino

October 15, 1984

PROSPECT, Ky. – Nearly every afternoon, on a rustic country lane near the Ohio River in Oldham County, a palomino horse named Butterscotch goes for a drive in his modified 1960 Lincoln Continental.

It is an unbelievable sight, but absolutely for real.

The man behind it all is 80-year-old Hamilton Morris, Sr., or "Ham" as he is known by most. Morris is a lifelong horse trainer who bought the big palomino in the early 1970s.

"He was an outlaw, running on a southern Indiana farm," Morris said. "They couldn't break him; I offered them a price for him and they took it."

The rest of the story is simply amazing.

Within a few years, Butterscotch, with Morris on his back, was performing five-gaits without a bridle, and was driving a car without assistance, other than voice commands from Morris, who walks a few feet behind the vehicle.

The car's top has been removed, and its seats have been replaced with a wooden floor and a metal-rail enclosure where Butterscotch stands. He enters and exits the vehicle on a ramp that slides from under the floor.

Except for the large brake and accelerator pedals on the floor, all of the car's controls – fitted with various lengths of soft rubber hose – have been elevated to mouth level. The steering wheel, starter, gearshift, horn, a

149

tape player and siren are all manipulated by the horse. Soon, a windshield wiper switch will be added.

Butterscotch enters the car on command, starts it, puts it in gear and off he goes.

He usually turns on the tape player and sounds the siren without being told. His speed varies from slow idle to a fast idle, but he rarely presses the brake or accelerator without being instructed to do so.

His trips normally cover a total of about 500 yards, from the paddock area near the barn where he is kept, down a narrow gravel road that leads past the Morris home. He turns the car around by himself in a large, grassy field, then guides it back onto the road and returns to the barn area.

Throughout the trip Butterscotch responds to his trainer's commands to "get back in the middle of the road," "cut," "come back," "get your foot on the gas," "brake," and a variety of other instructions typical of backseat drivers. He turns the large, padded steering wheel with his nose.

In addition to his driving skills, Butterscotch is toilet trained, and turns the light on and off in his stall.

Morris and Butterscotch have only one serious difference of opinion – the horse likes country music and Morris doesn't.

"Country music kinda worries me," Morris said. "One song, I broke the tape right up there at that tree. It was a song called 'She'll Be Coming 'Round the Mountain When She Comes.' He'd play that over and over again. My head got to roaring so bad I couldn't stand it."

"I want to get one of 'My Old Kentucky Home,' and try to wean him away from that country, you see."

Camera crews from "Real People," "You Asked for It," and numerous other television shows have visited Pond Creek Farm, where Morris is a trainer, to film his horse in action. His most recent media visitor was a reporter/photographer from the British newspaper, London Express.

Morris won't talk much about how he trained the horse, only that Butterscotch was "a fast learner."

"The horse has the ability to drive five miles without a bobble, if he's on a real good road," Morris said. "He drove in a whole parade over in southern Indiana a couple of years ago."

Footnote: I lost track of Ham Morris and Butterscotch after a few years, but they did appear on several network television shows.

PART THREE:

Names, Games & Flashes of Fame

Louisville's Other Greatest

November 25, 2005

RUDELL Stitch might never have won an Olympic gold boxing medal, a world title belt or the Medal of Freedom that was recently bestowed on his friend, Muhammad Ali. Yet the Louisville welterweight, who worked at a meatpacking house and rose to No. 2 in the world rankings in early 1960, earned a distinction that even "The Greatest" is unlikely to achieve:

Stitch was one of only four people in the past century to be awarded two Carnegie Hero Medals for risking his life to save another.

The fighter drowned in the summer of 1960 at age 27 when he deliberately swam back into a swirling Ohio River current in an effort to save his friend, Charles Oliver, after Oliver slipped from a ledge at the McAlpine lock and pulled Stitch in with him.

"Rudell was swimming toward shore and Charlie started yelling, and Rudell turned around and went back to get him," recalled Rich Keeling, Stitch's longtime friend. The drowning 6-foot, 180-pound Oliver still had on his waders when he grabbed the 5-foot 8-inch, 146-pound Stitch, and they disappeared.

In 1958, Stitch, the father of five boys and one girl, had rescued a stranger, Army Corps of Engineers worker Joseph Shifcar of Elizabeth, Ind., after Shifcar fell into the river near the same site. Stitch's oldest child, Donald, still has the fighter's Carnegie Hero Medals, his boxing robe, several scrapbooks of clippings and photographs, and a few precious memories of his parents.

Donald was only nine when his father died. The children lost their mother, Rosa, just four years later.

"Our grandmother came down from Detroit when our father died, and after my mother passed, she just kept all of us together at the house there instead of us getting separated. She took us to church, worked day work, got Social Security, and we never wanted for anything. The lights were never turned out," Donald Stitch remembered.

Donald's youngest brother, Daryl, later fought in the Golden Gloves, but Donald found football much more to his liking and earned a scholarship to Jackson State University.

Although Donald Stitch really hasn't recovered from the early loss of his parents, he has a wonderful legacy of his father that sportswriters, fighters and other fans of the sport have preserved over the decades, including one of the most revealing episodes of Stitch's short but brilliant 27-7 pro career.

PHOTO FROM FAMILY ARCHIVES

Boxing welterweight, Rudell Stitch.

"In the third round of his fight with Gaspar Ortega in Madison Square Garden, they accidentally butted heads," said Mickey Clark of the Louisville Sports Report, a friend of the boxer. "Rudell wasn't hurt, but Ortega was staggering around, and Rudell sort of backed away and wouldn't continue to hit him."

Stitch, who was leading the fight on points at the time, later told Clark that he never believed in taking advantage of an opponent during a head-butt. Although Ortega would win a decision, Stitch's action helped define his integrity in the boxing world as a fighter in a class all his own. Clark, Keeling, and numerous others who revere Stitch's contributions to boxing and to humanity, hope that somewhere in Louisville's new Muhammad Ali Center, space can one day be found for an exhibit commemorating the fighter.

A Bible verse that Stitch, a member of the Hope Presbyterian Church, had doubtless heard many times in his young life is cradled along the gilded edges of his two Carnegie Hero Medals, "Greater love hath no man than this; that a man lay down his life for his friends."

In that elite class of heroes, Rudell Stitch is among the greatest.

King Kelly Coleman

March 11, 2007

THE King may have left the building, but a piece of his heart is still there.

"King" Kelly Coleman, often described as "Kentucky's greatest basketball legend," is leading an effort to buy the old Wayland High School gym in Floyd County. That's where he once scored 75 points and pulled down 41 rebounds for the Wayland Wasps in a 1956 game against archrival Maytown.

Coleman, 68, who now lives just down the street from the gym, has pitched in to help the Wayland Historical Society buy the property for creation of an "Eastern Kentucky Sports Hall of Fame."

"In most of these small towns, the old schools have pretty much been razed and are gone," Coleman said. "We came up with an idea for a hall of fame just for mountain people, and we need all the help we can get."

The gym was the heart of the declining coal town in Coleman's teenage years. Beyond basketball, it served as the gathering place for nearly all school and community events outside of church. And at basketball games, sometimes 200 people would be turned away after 800 had crammed inside.

Many were there to watch Coleman, who had been cut from the B-team as an eighth-grader but practiced on a dirt court until he became a true basketball phenomenon. The long story of his becoming a small college All-American at Kentucky Wesleyan in Owensboro and being drafted by the NBA's New York Knicks could have ended with a glorious pro career. Instead, Coleman said, his self-destructive lifestyle ended his pro career almost before he had a chance to prove himself as a player.

He did lead the old American Basketball League in three-point scoring during the ABL's last season, playing for the Chicago Majors.

During his years at Wayland, sportswriters had quoted University of Kentucky coach Adolph Rupp as saying that Coleman was the best high school player he'd ever seen. And even today, former UK star Larry Conley, now a network basketball analyst, calls Coleman "arguably the best high school player to ever have played the game of basketball in the Bluegrass." In the 1956 state tournament, Coleman scored 68 points against Bell County.

Tourists still stop in Wayland wanting to see where "King Kelly," the shy, 6-foot-3-inch son of a coal miner and one of 11 children, averaged 46.8 points a game one season and etched his name on several pages of Kentucky's high school record books.

The recently published biography "King Kelly Coleman – Kentucky's greatest basketball legend," by Gary West (Acclaim Press), has spurred renewed interest in Coleman's amazing story and in dozens of other great basketball players and teams from the mountains.

Freddie James of the Prestonsburg tourism office believes there is enough interest in the outstanding mountain teams of yesteryear that a high school gymnasium trail could be developed for travelers among a number of the once-booming Eastern Kentucky coal towns whose old high school gyms remain.

David King, who owns Wayland gym, is negotiating a price with the historical society. He now rents the building for $35 an hour to local groups for pickup games. But the King is not there.

"They're always asking me to play," Coleman said. "But I don't think they understand that at 68 years old, a basketball court is no place to be."

"I was always comfortable in that gym," he remembered, "and it just seemed like anywhere I got the ball, even if it was at the other end of the court, I felt I could make it from there. I used to even shoot jump shots in practice with my eyes closed just to see how close I could come, and surprisingly I would make several."

The Wayland Historical Society is hoping that if the old gym can be bought, King Kelly might be persuaded to drop by occasionally to share a few stories with visitors.

Kelly Coleman

Kelly drives in for a layup against Bell County in the 1956 state tournament consolation game.

PHOTO FROM HUGHES COLLECTION

Patrick Henry Hughes

September 17, 2006

Y OU had to love the great Cardinal defense, clutch air strikes and a few dazzling individual moves during the University of Louisville's win last night, but did you see the reverse spin maneuver that trumpet player Patrick Henry Hughes and his father pulled off during the band's halftime show? Whooaaa Nellie!

The Hughes halftime tandem, Patrick the son playing trumpet from his wheelchair in the U of L marching band, while Patrick the father pushes, has been making amazing team plays for most of the younger Patrick's 18 years.

Soon after Patrick was born, without eyes and unable to straighten his arms and legs, his father discovered a unique way of stopping him from crying.

"He would lay me on top of the piano and play something," Patrick said. "We don't know whether I loved it or what, but I immediately got quiet." Seldom has Patrick been quiet around musical instruments since then.

By nine months old he was plunking on the piano keys from his high chair, and at two years old he was playing children's songs on the piano that he had learned from his Sesame Street tapes.

His mastery of piano and voice has since earned him performances at the Kennedy Center, in international arts festivals and on network television.

161

When the former all-state trumpeter at Louisville's Atherton High School asked U of L band director Greg Byrne if he could join the university's pep band, he was surprised when Byrne told him yes, but that all pep band members were also required to be in the marching band.

"To my delight and surprise he put Patrick right there with the rest of the trumpet section, and we're out there rolling with the rest of the band doing all the formations," Patrick's father said. "It's a little bit of a workout, but it's been a lot of fun."

The senior Hughes works a part time night shift at UPS to give himself time for taking Patrick to band practices and to classes at U of L, where he is a Spanish major. The father, a 45-year-old former U of L violin major, and his wife, Patricia, have two younger sons, Cameron and Jesse.

His father attends all of Patrick's rehearsals and mans the wheelchair during marching band events. Although he usually wears black and red for halftime shows, he doesn't suit up in a band uniform.

"It means I don't have to march in step, but I try," he joked. "My job is to get Patrick to the right place at the right time." Sometimes during the intricate maneuvers of the 214-member band, the halftime show gets a bit tricky.

"One formation we do is called the 'Gladiator,' where the band splits into two blocks and the blocks march toward each other and mesh, then we go into a diamond shape, pretty fast-paced," his father said. "I lean Patrick back on just his back wheels and make the cuts and turns, and hopefully we don't run over any of the trombone players."

A friend of the Hughes family, Dave Fuchs, helped Patrick's dad modify some wheels from Patrick's old red Radio-Flyer wagon that were placed on the front of the wheelchair to make it handle more easily.

The University of Louisville has a slogan: "Dare to be Great." Sometimes its greatness surfaces in the classrooms or its sports teams, and sometimes in obscure little triumphs of will over adversity.

During yesterday's halftime show a blind trumpet player, riding in a wheelchair pushed by his father, made a reverse spin move on two wheels during the band's "Gladiator" formation, and no one missed a beat.

Footnote: The follow-up notes on this story have already been mentioned in this book's foreword by my son, Eric, a sports columnist for The Courier-Journal.

Mr. Wildcat's Night

April 4, 2008

L EXINGTON, Ky. – "The House that Rupp Built" belonged only
to Bill Keightley last night.

After 48 years of his sitting on the sidelines, the sanctuary of
Kentucky basketball yielded center court to "Mr. Wildcat" for two hours
on this deep blue evening in the heart of the Bluegrass.

A wave of memories and emotions swept the somber throng of about
3,000 fans and current and former players and coaches surrounding Bill
Keightley's flag-draped casket. Overhead hung
the retired Kentucky jersey bearing his
name. A large blue bow marked his chair
on the sideline.

For all of its glory, tradition and
mystique, Wildcat Nation's farewell
to its 81-year-old equipment manager may have more perfectly em-
bodied the heart and soul of Kentucky's incredible love for UK basketball than any singular event over
decades of the school's history.

Some 1,200 mourners from the
mountains of Eastern Kentucky to the
bayous of the Western Purchase had filed

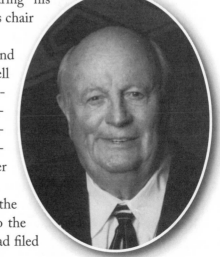

UNIVERSITY OF KENTUCKY

past his casket earlier in the day to pay their respects to the man whose job title was "equipment manager," but whose popularity had made him a true Kentucky treasure.

During his nearly half-century on the UK bench, from the Adolph Rupp years to Billy Gillispie, Keightley became the personification of loyalty to the program, keeper of the transcendent Big Blue spirit through thick and thin.

He was a fixture on the Kentucky bench for nearly 1,500 games and thousands of practices, what former UK great Kyle Macy called a "true link between the generations of Kentucky basketball."

Keightley was the most famous equipment manager in America, revered by many of the college game's celebrated coaches, players and broadcasters. Referee Gerald Boudreaux often would bow in his presence.

Everywhere he went, people wanted to shake his hand and get his autograph or picture. "Mr. Wildcat" happily obliged with a trademark smile, and usually a personal story that made the souvenir all the more memorable.

His most endearing trait may have been his innate understanding of Kentuckians and their love affair with the Wildcats. Keightley grew up on a dairy farm in Anderson County and was all-state honorable mention in basketball at the old Kavanaugh High School, whose tiny gym is still standing in Lawrenceburg.

Like most other Kentuckians of that era, he was drawn to UK's basketball through radio broadcasts of the games long before television brought them into living rooms. He was a Marine during WWII, then a mail carrier in Lexington.

Bill Keightley was one of us. He just happened to have a seat on the UK bench at every game. UK fans saw in his face the reflections of their own joy and pain through victory and defeat. Keightley was the only man I've ever seen who could smile and grimace simultaneously, which often came in handy on the Kentucky bench.

He was, for many UK fans, players and even coaches, a living Big Blue security blanket, always within reach during the Wildcats' brightest or darkest hours.

Rules of the game, uniforms, players, coaches, broadcasters and even gyms changed. But Keightley was the one constant in UK basketball.

Rest easy, Bill. There will always be a place for the spirit of "Mr. Wildcat" on the Kentucky bench.

Lincoln Lifesaver

March 12, 1990

THE way Barry Thomas sees it, had it not been for Austin Gollaher – his great-great-great-grandfather – Abraham Lincoln
might have been lost to the world before anyone ever heard of
him. "That's stretching it, I guess … but honestly, it's not that far from the
truth," said Thomas, 27, who operates a swimming-pool service business
in Louisville. History is rather vague about Lincoln's boyhood in Kentucky, but there is a lasting tale that Gollaher, who was born in 1806 and
died in 1898, rescued Abe from flood-swollen Knob Creek in a section
which then was in Hardin and now is in LaRue County.

In the first year of his presidency, Lincoln is said to have told a White
House visitor, Dr. Jesse Rodman of Hodgenville, Ky.: "Jesse, I wouldn't be
here today if Austin Gollaher hadn't once fished me out of Knob Creek.
I was 8 at the time and Austin was 11. I must have been three-quarters
drowned when he dragged me up on the bank."

The incident, although ignored in some Lincoln histories, appears in
several credible biographies. Marilyn Tolbert, librarian at the The Lincoln
Museum in Fort Wayne, Ind., repository of the largest private Lincoln
collection in the nation, said she believes the story is generally accepted
by historians.

The book "Lincoln Day by Day," a publication of the Lincoln Sesqui-
centennial Commission, notes that the tale "is one of the few stories of
Lincoln's boyhood in Kentucky which may be factual."

Lincoln's one-time law partner, William H. Herndon, included the story in his "Herndon's Life of Lincoln."

He said Gollaher told him in 1865 that he and Lincoln were trying to slide on a log across Knob Creek when the incident occurred.

"The boys were in pursuit of birds (another account says an opossum) when young Lincoln fell into the water, and his vigilant companion, who survives to narrate the charming story, fished him out with a sycamore branch," Herndon wrote.

Barry Thomas' grandmother, 83-year-old Rose Thomas of Louisville, who has helped her grandson with much of the family history, said she doesn't remember hearing much talk in the family about Gollaher's heroics "until some of the older ones began to die off."

In John Rogers Gore's "The Boyhood of Abraham Lincoln," Gollaher, in later life, related several instances in which he and Lincoln had narrowly escaped serious injury or even possible death when they were playmates, including the time a boulder fell off a cliff and landed where the two had been playing only seconds earlier.

"God watched over Abe Lincoln," Gollaher declared, according to the book. "He didn't want him killed because there were no others like him, and he wanted to use Abe for a big purpose, and he didn't want to go to the trouble to make another like him...

"And don't you know that I got it into my child head that God was watching over me, too, so that I could keep Abe company and amuse him with my antics. When I was with Abe, I had a sort of safe and secure feeling, a feeling that nothing of any serious consequence could happen to either of us...

Barry Thomas holds a picture of his great-great-great-grandfather, Austin Gollaher.

PHOTO BY BYRON CRAWFORD

"It was no surprise to me when I heard Abe had been elected president. I reckon I saved Abe's life two or three times, but if I hadn't been there, God would have saved him some other way."

The only memento Gollaher ever received for saving Lincoln's life – a gold-headed, cedar walking stick, cut from a tree on the old Lincoln farm – was presented to him in a public tribute by the citizens of Hodgenville in the 1880s. Its whereabouts now are unknown.

Gollaher said he had once been invited to the White House by Lincoln, but declined because he was afraid to ride in trains.

He spent his life as a farmer on Knob Creek, where he married Polly Price, a local girl. The couple had six children. Gollaher was an elder in Pleasant Grove Baptist Church and served for a time as a justice of the peace. He is buried under a simple marker that bears the inscription "Lincoln's Playmate," in the Pleasant Grove Church Cemetery at White City in LaRue County.

Every few years, some of his descendants gather at Lincoln's boyhood home for a reunion and a visit to the cemetery, where several family members are buried near the grave of the family hero. "I'm not married, and I don't see myself being married in the near future," Barry Thomas said. "But I figure if I ever have a son I might want to name him Austin Gollaher Thomas."

Kentucky's Mister Sandman

November 13, 1996

VERSAILLES, Ky. – The giant sandbox behind Damon Farmer's Shadetree Studio in Woodford County serves a grand purpose. Farmer, 47, is the world's champion sand sculptor.

A computer animator for Studio Link in Lexington, he earned the championship several weeks ago in British Columbia during competition among 20 of the best sand sculptors in the world. Each artist was given 22 hours to complete his or her work.

When Farmer finished he had produced a remarkable eight-foot-tall scene from Jack and the Beanstalk. The sculpture won not only the championship but also the People's Choice Award from an appreciative audience of thousands. Farmer was second in the world competition last year and has twice placed third.

Unlike the small sand castles that many of us have built on the beach, most of Farmer's sand sculptures are reminiscent of the flowing drapery and graceful postures used by ancient Greek sculptors, or of the Renaissance works of the French and Italian masters.

"I started this about 20 years ago while I was an art student at Berea College," Farmer said. "It was just a vacation at the beach, really, about the first time I had ever been. We'd been out on Santa Rosa Island, Fla., to see the Civil War fort there ... and I just thought I'd reproduce the fort."

Soon Farmer was expressing his talents in an old and natural, yet often overlooked, medium. He has left a 50-ton sand sculpture of Christopher Columbus on a beach in Fort Lauderdale, Fla. He left a knight and a dragon on the beach at South Padre Island, Texas. He was commissioned to do a 15-foot-tall sculpture of the history of Iowa at the Iowa State Fair this year, and to do a herd of horses at the Minnesota State Fair. His sculptures - mostly vanished now - number in the hundreds.

"You're starting with basically ... a blank canvas in the morning, and by the end of the day you're opening your gallery. Then it's all gone," Farmer said.

Although some of his fellow artists specialize only in sand castles, Farmer prefers human and animal forms that express emotion and whimsy.

He has sculpted scenes from The Wizard of Oz. At the Super Bowl he sculpted TV commentators Al Michaels, Frank Gifford and Dan Dierdorf.

"There is a lot of freedom in sand," he said. "It's always like a magic

FARMER COLLECTION

169

slate. You do whatever you want to do, and learn from the process, then the next day you start all over. For the sculptor, the process is a lot of it, and the sand makes you focus on the process to a large degree, because that's pretty much it in the end. Except you have the photos to remind yourself of what you did."

While most of his sand sculptures last only a few days, some are sprayed with a biodegradable coating that can preserve them for several weeks for large exhibits.

"A lot of the appeal for me in this medium is that it is so environmentally friendly," Farmer said. "It's something you can do without any chemicals, without using any electricity ... anybody can go to the beach and use the sand and the water that's there and make beautiful pieces, if they'll spend the time."

Gone With The Wind

Summer, 1980

OWENSBORO, Ky. – Since his Hollywood days, John Friedmann Jr. has lived in such seclusion that even some of his
neighbors in Owensboro are not aware that in 1938 Friedmann
helped create costumes for one of the greatest motion pictures of all time
– "Gone With the Wind."

Friedmann retains a wealth of memories and trivia from his work as an
assistant to costume designer Walter Plunkett on the film classic.

Did you know that the famous green velvet dress that Scarlett O'Hara
fashioned from one of the drapes at Tara weighed 40 pounds?

"And that was using a lighter-weight velvet than what the real cur-
tains weighed," Friedmann said. "If we'd have used the actual velvet in the
drapery it would have weighed about 80 pounds."

From the beginning, he recalled, nearly everyone who worked on the
picture sensed that they were involved with something special. But they
could scarcely have imagined that it was destined to become the gold
standard of cinematic excellence.

Friedmann described the picture's producer, the late David O. Selznick,
as "an ogre."

He recounts costume designers spending days designing gowns and
other clothing, only to watch Selznick often thumb through 50 design
sketches in a matter of seconds before dismissing them as worthless, and
treatening to fire the designers if they didn't do better.

171

Designers finally devised a new approach.

"They'd submit a few absolutely awful sketches, mixed in with a few that they felt were very good," said Friedmann. Selznick would invariably choose one of the good ones, sometimes telling the designers, "Now, do you see what can do when you really try?"

Friedmann remembers a charming Georgia woman of about 33, named Marian Dabney, a department head in the design group, who personified Selznick's ideal character for the role of Scarlett O'Hara.

"She had wind-blown black hair, a sparkling personality, and Selznick was quoted as saying that Marian would be Scarlett if she were only 10 years younger."

"This was way before all the publicity screen tests," Friedmann said. "Vivien Leigh proved to be a 'sister' (to Marian Dabney) in appearance, upturned eyes and all."

There was behind-the-scenes talk that Clark Gable, at age 36, might be too old for the part of Rhett Butler.

Friedmann never heard Vivien Leigh complain, although he said she often worked 12 and 14 hours or more on many days during the approximately 200 days of filming. He said that she sometimes had to stand for a half-hour as three or four costume workers made adjustments to her gowns.

"When there would be early filming, a girl would be stationed with Vivien Leigh in her sleeping quarters the night before to make sure she didn't sleep on her face and leave wrinkles that would spoil the shots."

During the course of the picture, fatigue took its toll on the actress, Friedmann said. She lost weight and was sometimes sickly and weak. He believes that makers of the film chose many instances when she was actually ill to shoot scenes of Scarlett in her lowest moments.

In addition to his costume design work, Friedmann was also in charge of "aging" Scarlett's dresses to make them look properly faded and worn as the epic film progressed. This was done by soaking the garments in various mixtures of bleach, turning them inside out, using real Georgia clay and red pigment to soil the garments, and chalk and oil for sweat.

Remember the Union soldier Scarlett shot in the face at Tara? Friedmann said that the actor who played that soldier later committed suicide by shooting himself in the face.

Friedmann still hears some news of cast members and other workers on the film through occasional correspondence with actresses Olivia de Havilland and Butterfly McQueen, the latter of whom became a French teacher after "Gone With the Wind."

Friedmann later assisted with costumes on another Selznick production, "Rebecca," Alfred Hitchcock's Hollywood directing debut.

Costume designer Walter Plunkett's later works included Academy Award winning designs for "An American in Paris."

But for most who had worked on "Gone With the Wind," nothing could ever match the excitement and spectacle of having worked on the greatest motion picture of its era and one of the best of all time.

John Friedmann saved a few mementoes. From each costume made for all of the principal roles in "Gone With the Wind," he saved a swatch of material and sent it to his mother back in Owensboro. From those scraps of cloth she made a "Gone With the Wind" quilt in which she depicted each character wearing a costume made from the actual fabric used for his or her costume in the film. Friedmann still has his valuable keepsake quilt today.

It reminds him of the nearly 6,000 separate costume items designed for the 2,500 member cast, and of the 750,000 manhours spent in production.

"Gone With the Wind," but never forgotten.

Footnote: John Friedmann Jr. died a few years after this story appeared. His quilt is now the property of a relative in Atlanta. It was exhibited at the Margaret Mitchell Museum in Atlanta during the 50th Anniversary of the motion picture, in 1989.

Friedmann, holding the "Gone With the Wind" quilt, has some pieces of Vivien Leigh's calico dress and fabrics from other costumes draped over his shoulders.

Harlan Globetrotters

May 8, 2005

SURE you know the Harlem Globetrotters, but do you know the Harlan Globetrotters?

That's Harlan - as in Harlan County, Ky. - the place famous for coal and the natural beauty of Black Mountain and Blanton Forest.

The rugged coal camps of Harlan County have produced many notable individuals, including three Harlem Globetrotters in different eras - the late Willis Thomas and Paul "Showtime" Gaffney, as well as Bernie Bickerstaff, who briefly joined the Globetrotters before choosing a path that led to a coaching career in the National Basketball Association.

All three men are children of Harlan County coal miners.

Thomas died just over two years ago at age 70 and is buried in Laurel County, Ky.

Bickerstaff, who later served as basketball director for the Globetrotters and coached a Globetrotters touring squad for about three years, has been head coach in Seattle, Denver and Washington, and currently is coach and general manager of the NBA Charlotte Bobcats.

Gaffney, who lives in Houston, is the current "Clown Prince" of the Globetrotters, and is in his 12th season as successor to the great Meadowlark Lemon.

"They say where you come from doesn't matter, but it really does matter," Gaffney explained. "It really sets your standards. ... I mean who works harder than people in the coal mines? It was just bred in you to work hard."

174

FAMILY ARCHIVES

Gaffney with Dan Rather

Thomas and Gaffney grew up in Lynch, while Bickerstaff lived in neighboring Benham and even worked briefly in a coal mine before playing and coaching at San Diego State, then moving to the pro ranks.

"People talk about the NBA being tough, but I tell them that's light-weight compared to where I grew up," Bickerstaff once told a reporter. "But the one good thing we had there was nurturing, and you knew that the people there were in your corner."

Thomas attended Tennessee State University on a basketball scholar-ship and was discovered there by scouts of the Globetrotters, for whom he played seven seasons. His wife, Barbara, who now lives in the rural Laurel County community of East Bernstadt, said her husband worked as a teacher in Chicago after leaving the Globetrotters and before the couple retired to Laurel County.

"When we were in Chicago, my husband kept in touch with people from Kentucky ... and sometimes we would come back to Harlan twice a year," she said.

Gaffney recalls that as a youngster he made a copy superimposing a photo of his face on that of a professional basketball star in a sports magazine.

"I had to see myself as a professional athlete and work hard and do the things that I needed to do to make it to the next level," he explained.

Gaffney's story offers a great lesson for youngsters today who, in order to overcome barriers and attain ambitious goals, often need to visualize themselves as successful in a chosen profession, said Bill Turner, a native of Lynch who now is vice president for university initiatives at the University of Kentucky.

Willis "Bunny" Thomas

Bernie Bickerstaff

"Paul putting it that way is the lesson of a lot of us," said Turner. "Mine was, 'I wonder what's over that mountain right there?' You know, in Eastern Kentucky, if you go over one mountain you'll see there's another mountain. Peaks and valleys. I think in some sense the story of life is, you get over one mountain and think you've achieved something, then you say, 'I think I can make it over the next one.'

"You should come to Harlan County Memorial Day weekend," Turner added. "The black population will quadruple, because everybody comes home to decorate the graves."

Airport Voices

May 4, 2008

THOSE of you who are flying out of Louisville will take two of our voices with you almost wherever you go. "While on the moving sidewalk, please stand to the right so others can pass ..."
Two of the most prominent airport voices in the world, those of former Louisville broadcasters Jack Fox and Carolyn Hopkins, originate at the studios of Louisville's Innovative Electronic Designs.

"They're primarily the voices we've used all through the years since the mid 1980s," said Hardy Martin, president of IED. "We're in 82 of the top 100 U.S. and Canadian airports and other airports all over the world from Paris to Tel Aviv to Honolulu."

The company's announcement control systems serve New York and Chicago subway passengers, and emergency evacuation networks on Capitol Hill and at the Pentagon, Marshall Space Flight Center, Kennedy Space Center and many other facilities.

Martin and his lifelong friend and business partner, Ray Allen, now chief financial officer of the company, organized and performed with the locally popular "Carnations and Tren-Dells" band and vocal group when they were in high school during the 1950s and '60s in Louisville. They later founded two talent agencies, Allen-Martin Productions and an audio console firm.

The 100 employees of IED LLC have pioneered the sophisticated announcement control systems for not only millions of subway and airport travelers, but visitors to the Mayo Clinic and some of the world's largest convention centers. Jack Fox, a former announcer at WHAS Radio in Louisville, and Carolyn Hopkins, who formerly worked for WAKY and WKLO in Louisville, are the company's trademark voices.

"'Smoking is permitted in designated areas only; please refrain from smoking while walking throughout the building.' That's the one that I usually use if somebody wants to hear the voice," said Hopkins.

Late one night on an airport moving sidewalk between flights, Hopkins was behind a man who was blocking the sidewalk just as her voice came on the terminal speaker urging people to stand to the right.

"I repeated it word for word behind him, hoping it would make a difference, but he just stood there like 'Huh?'"

Fox says his "May I have your attention, please? This area is for loading and unloading only" and his "moving sidewalk" announcements are the ones most requested by friends.

When his granddaughter, Ruby, was about four years old, she was waiting with Fox at an airport baggage claim carousel where his voice kept repeating, "arriving passengers please pick up baggage at carousel ..."

Ruby finally turned to her mother and asked, "Why is Grandpa talking so much?"

Wright Bros. Chauffeur

January 7, 1985

L ANCASTER, Ky. – If he had it to do over, he'd nose into things a little more, 96-year-old Frank Conn said of his brush with two giants in American aviation history.

For about one week each year, "somewhere around 1910, 1911 and 1912," Conn was a chauffeur for Orville and Wilbur Wright.

As a teenager in the early 1900s, he left his home in the rural Garrard County community of Paint Lick to fulfill his dream of becoming a steam locomotive engineer. But on the way to apply for a job with the railroad, he ran into his cousin, a chauffeur for a wealthy Cincinnati tobacco dealer, who persuaded him to go to Cincinnati and take automobile mechanic's training instead.

Conn worked a year and a half with a mechanic in Cincinnati, then found a job at the Overland Motor Co. of Indianapolis where he spent the next five years.

It was there, he said, that he was often summoned from his job in the shop to chauffeur for Overland's president, John Willys, later the father of the Willys Whippet automobile and the Willys Jeep.

"See, Willys had two big old cars, limousines, a Pope Toledo and Pope Hartford, chain-driven; had chains and sprockets on 'em," Conn recalled. "When some visitors would come in, they'd act big and get me as a driver. I don't know, they'd just taken a liking to me some way or another."

So it was that when the Wright Brothers brought one of their early

179

planes to Indianapolis for an exhibit at the Indianapolis 500 Speedway. Willys, a long-time friend of the Wrights, dispatched Conn to drive them around in one of the limousines.

"I drove them the first year. Then the second year they came back, the Wright brothers asked Willys to get the same chauffeur," Conn said. "I went and stayed with them at the hotel, and ate with them. They'd stay a whole week."

During exhibition flights in Indianapolis, Conn said, the plane was seldom flown more than 500-600 feet at

about 30 miles per hour, 35-40 feet off the ground. It was generally piloted by a fellow Conn knew only as "Bombo," who traveled with the Wrights.

"They were nice people," Conn said. "They stayed together practically all the time. One of them was about six feet or six feet two inches, and the other was about five-eight."

Wilbur and Orville never tipped him, Conn said, but they did tell him once that they'd like to have him as a full-time chauffeur if they could afford it.

Conn said that he was allowed to sit in the airplane several times, but that guards stood watch over the plane around the clock.

"There were some more starting to build planes, and they didn't let anybody get too close to it," he said. In fact, Conn remembers that the Wright brothers and Glenn Curtiss, another pioneer airplane builder, nearly had a fight once in Indianapolis, because the Wrights believed Curtiss was trying to steal some of their ideas.

He didn't realize at the time that history was being made, Conn lamented, and he has not a single picture or memento to prove his chauffeur's story.

However, Patrick Nolan, professor of history and director of archives and special collections at Wright State University in Dayton, Ohio, has no doubt that Conn is close to correct on all of his recollections.

Nolan's research on the Wright brothers suggests that they may have made several trips to Indianapolis, and it is plausible to believe that they had a driver while there, Nolan said.

Frank Conn returned to Lancaster before World War I and, following service in the war, started his first garage there in 1919. He retired as a mechanic in 1973, but he still walks to his old garage every day and spends a few hours sitting at his antique roll-top desk, contemplating the swift passage of time and occasionally sharing with a visitor the story of how he once chauffeured the fathers of aviation.

Footnote: Frank Conn died in October, 1985, nine months after this story was published, and ten days short of his 97th birthday. His great-niece, Margaret Burkett of Garrard County, found two unlabeled photographs among his possessions; one of a very early airplane sitting in a field and another of a small group of men sitting on the ground. Two of them appear to be the Wright brothers.

Krispy Kreme Beginning?

December 31, 2000

KRISPY Kreme doughnuts may owe much of their sweet success to onetime Paducah resident and former Belle of Louisville first mate Joe LeBoeuf, who died in Louisville in May, 1999, apparently unware that Krispy Kremes might have started with his recipe. The story gets about as sticky as a kettle of hot glaze.

Krispy Kreme has for years said that in 1933 Vernon Rudolph, the founder of Krispy Kreme, bought a doughnut shop in Paducah from a French chef from New Orleans named Joe LeBeau, and that Rudolph received the company's assets, goodwill, and the rights to a secret, yeast-raised doughnut recipe.

Soon after acquiring the recipe, Rudolph and his partner moved to Nashville, Tennessee, and in 1937 relocated to Winston-Salem, North Carolina, the company's current headquarters.

Early this year, Paducah historian Barron White, author of "I Remember Paducah When ..." (McClanahan Publishing) began researching Paducah's Krispy Kreme connection after reading a Smithsonian magazine article that mentioned Joe LeBeau as the French chef with whom the recipe originated.

Old Paducah city directories yielded no Joe LeBeau, but did list a Joe LeBoeuf, whose Broad Street address matched that of the purported doughnut shop. White was able to find LeBoeuf's obituary and to locate his widow, Irma, 86, and oldest daughter, Anna Dean Haueter, who both

182

Joe LeBoeuf, ca. 1970s.

still live in the Shively area of Jefferson County.

Ironically, none of Le-Boeuf's family had ever heard the Krispy Kreme story, and they doubt that Joe, who died at age 93, ever knew that his recipe may have grown into the Krispy Kreme doughnut empire.

LeBoeuf grew up in Lake Charles, Louisiana, and began work as a cook and deckhand on an Army Corps of Engineers dredge boat at age 16. He was transferred to Paducah in the early 1930s, where he and his young family made their home until 1949, when he was transferred to Louisville.

His family said he never owned a doughnut shop, never mentioned the Krispy Kreme recipe, and never, to their knowledge, was paid for the formula.

He was, however, an excellent cook who often made doughnuts at home using his own closely guarded recipe. Furthermore, his family says, he loved Krispy Kreme doughnuts and, even toward the end of his life, when cancer had robbed him of his appetite for most other foods, he often asked for Krispy Kremes.

"He would always say, 'That's the best doughnut I ever ate,'" recalled daughter Judy Thompson.

Based on information from old Krispy Kreme documents, White and the LeBoeuf family theorize that Joe LeBoeuf probably gave his dough-nut recipe to a Paducah grocer named Ishmael Armstrong, an uncle of Vernon Rudolph, the founder of Krispy Kreme. Rudolph soon moved away and began selling the doughnuts in other states, and LeBoeuf never associated the Krispy Kreme name with his recipe.

"He could have discovered America and he never would have told a soul," said daughter, Sue Gill. "That's the kind of man he was."

One of the most telling clues that Joe LeBoeuf may have originated the Krispy Kreme recipe was revealed several months ago when Carver Rudolph of Winston-Salem, a son of the Krispy Kreme founder, compared recipe notes with LeBoeuf's family and discovered that two of the secret ingredients and one of the preparation techniques used by LeBoeuf were the same as those used in the original Krispy Kreme formula.

"Personally, I would just like people to know of his connection with Krispy Kreme," said LeBoeuf's youngest daughter, Joan Kruse.

The family also hopes that the Smithsonian Institution will correct the spelling of his name from "LeBeau" to "LeBoeuf" in its Krispy Kreme exhibit, and that the Krispy Kreme Company will publicly set the record straight.

LeBoeuf's widow, Irma, said, "Maybe they'll send us a dozen doughnuts."

Pioneer Cave Guide

October 19, 2007

WHEN the light is right, you may still see dim letters spelling out "S-T-E-P-H-E-N" left by the smoke from a tallow candle on the ceiling of Mammoth Cave more than 150 years ago. Slave guide Stephen Bishop used a mirror to prevent candle wax from dripping into his eyes as he left his imprint on the giant cave he was exploring, and some of his S's are backward.

Yesterday, members of the Cave Research Foundation, who are holding their 50th annual meeting at Mammoth Cave National Park, paused during their tour of the same passageways that Bishop once charted to hear a few pages of his fascinating life story.

Tour leader Roger Brucker, co-author of "The Longest Cave" and author of the soon-to-be-published historical novel about Bishop's cave experiences, "Grand, Gloomy and Peculiar," frequently stopped to read excerpts from his manuscript and to share observations about Bishop's role in the cave's development.

"He's kind of *the* pioneer cave explorer in this country … and really the prototype of modern cave guiding," said Brucker, a founding director of the Cave Research Foundation. "He was the economic engine that put Mammoth Cave on the map between 1840 and 1855."

Bishop's winning personality, coupled with his knowledge of and obsession with the cave, made him easily the most popular guide of the era.

185

"He has occupied himself so frequently in exploring the various passages of the cavern that there is now no living being who knows it so well. The discoveries made have been the result of his courage, intelligence and untiring zeal," stated an account published in "Stephen Bishop, The Man and the Legend," by former cave historian Harold Meloy.

Bishop's first owner, Franklin Gorin of Glasgow, bought Mammoth Cave in 1838 and assigned the then 17-year-old Bishop to be a cave guide. In October 1839, when Gorin sold the cave to John Croghan, the owner of Locust Grove in Louisville, Bishop was sold as part of the cave and remained a guide.

"He was the first American cave explorer that we know about who was systematic in what he did," Brucker said. "He was so good at it that his owners wrote about his exploits to European papers and papers in New York, and he achieved some fame in his own time for his discoveries."

Croghan asked Bishop to sketch a map of the passages, which was published in a book called "Rambles in Mammoth Cave." The book became the basis for later guidebooks, and reprints may still be bought in the park gift shop.

Bishop's wife, Charlotte, was a manager of the Mammoth Cave Hotel dining room who had worked for Croghan at Locust Grove. Bishop died in 1857 and is buried in the Old Guides Cemetery on a ridge near the cave entrance. The Cave Research Foundation, which was founded 100 years after Bishop's death, continues to explore the 367 miles of known passageways in Mammoth Cave in the belief that natural connections will be found to many more miles of what already is the world's longest cave.

"It's within a few hundred feet of a 110-mile cave system called Fisher Ridge, and within several hundred feet of the Martin Ridge Cave system, which is about 32 miles long," Brucker said. "If those are connected, and some of us feel that's a certainty, that would put us over the 500-mile mark."

Stephen Bishop, they sure could use your help.

Miss America 1944

September 2, 1992

WAYNESBURG, Ky. – Even before I started liking girls, I liked Miss America, 1944.

I remember seeing Venus Ramey from a distance while passing her house when I was a boy. In those days she lived only a couple of miles up the road from our place in Lincoln County. Although I never saw her up close, I could tell from a distance that she was a knockout, and I secretly hoped that someday I would meet her.

Several days ago I called 67-year-old Venus Ramey at her farm in Lincoln County, introduced myself and asked if I could write a story about her. We met for lunch, and I saw her for the first time in more than 30 years.

She was driving a gray Ford pickup. Her outfit was a frumpled buttercup-yellow visor and a yellow skirt and blouse, with white sandals. She carried a leather briefcase that contained clippings and photos I had requested.

"I am so sorry," she said, realizing she was an hour late. "I don't have a watch."

Over the next two hours, I learned that she was born in Ashland, Ky., and had lived in Cincinnati and Paintsville as a child, but had grown up mostly in southern Lincoln County, where her family had a farm.

Her mother, a native of Paintsville, had gone to New York while pregnant and was so enamored of Broadway that she named her baby daughter Venus, in the hopes that the child's name would one day be written in lights.

The dream came true in Atlantic City, N.J., in 1944. Venus Ramey, representing the District of Columbia, where she had been working as a showgirl, was crowned Miss America. The five-foot six-and-a-half-inch, auburn-haired, blue-eyed beauty had won the swimsuit competition, was a consensus winner in evening gowns and had wowed the Atlantic City crowd with a rumba number in English and Spanish. Talent scouts from MGM and 20th Century Fox studios had already made appointments to talk with her, regardless of the pageant's outcome.

"I had already worked as a showgirl and a chorus girl and I wanted to get into show business," Ramey said. "But the pageant had tied up Miss 1943 and I for two years with Lever Bros. to go on a department store tour advertising Lux Flakes and some kind of cosmetics."

When Venus Ramey finally arrived in Hollywood, she did not like what she found.

"It wasn't because I didn't have opportunities. I met the right people, but I didn't like them," Ramey said. "Hollywood, for years, has been the red-light district of the United States, and that's putting it mildly."

Life in Hollywood's fast lane did not appeal to the girl who had grown up on a Kentucky farm, so after only a few months she gave up her attempts to break into motion pictures and returned to the life she had left. Her decision resulted in feature stories in Life magazine and other publications.

She ran unsuccessfully for Kentucky state representative in the 1950s, and in the late 1970s for City Council in Cincinnati, where she later published a community newspaper.

She was married once and has two sons and six grandchildren. But she is divorced and now lives alone, except for the dogs and cats, chickens, goats and a miniature horse that share her 70-acre farm in Lincoln County.

These days, she jokes that she was Miss America in 1910; she often wears bib overalls and she spends her spare time writing murder mysteries and other novels that she'd like to publish. Her hope was always

PHOTO BY BYRON CRAWFORD

to be a comic, she said, and she has written a comedy routine about her Miss America years that she may take on the road some day. She worries about the plight of family farms, and says she has taken up smoking to protest the anti-tobacco movement.

Among the most treasured mementos of her glamour years is a picture of a World War II, B-17 bomber of the U.S. Air Force's 301st Bombardment Group, with her picture and name on the nose. The 301st, which in 1945 was based in Foggia, Italy, chose Ramey as "the girl we'd most like to bail out with over a deserted Pacific isle."

Just this year she got a letter from one of the fliers, thanking her for an autographed picture and note she sent his outfit in 1945.

It was like the one she signed for me: "From Miss America, 1944."

Footnote: In April 2007, Venus Ramey made international news when she drew a .38 caliber pistol and shot out the tire of an intruder's vehicle near a storage building on her property from which several pieces of old farm equipment had previously been stolen. Balanced on her walker, the 82-year-old former Miss America held the suspect at gunpoint until sheriff's deputies arrived.

Elvis Car

November 24, 2006

WHILE Elvis Presley was in Louisville for a concert 50 years ago this week, he bought a new car and a color TV for his grandfather and step-grandmother, and delivered the gifts to their home in south Louisville.

"The King," his grandparents, and perhaps the TV are long departed. But the colonial white-over-mist-blue '57 Ford Fairlane is getting a tender loving makeover, except for its original steering wheel and mirror, in a Valley Station garage where it has been parked for many years.

"I finally found somebody that would come to my garage and paint it," said Charles Burney, who in 1982 split the $2,500 cost of the car with his father, C.W. Burney.

The Ford came with a hand written cardboard sign in the window declaring it to be an Elvis car, and a bill of sale from Riggs Motor Co. at 530 W. Broadway in Louisville, listing the original owner as "J.D. Pressley, 4008 Beaver St." in Louisville. But Burney was skeptical of its Elvis connection, as was the former owner in Louisville, who sold the car to settle the estate of a son.

Then Burney met a co-worker, Sandra Slater, at what then was Louisville Ordnance. She had been a neighbor and friend of Presley's grandparents, Jesse and Vera Pressley, in the Ashland Avenue area off Taylor Boulevard. She remembered when Elvis gave them the car.

Newspaper accounts indicate that Jesse Pressley, who once worked for

190

the Pepsi-Cola Bottling Co. in Louisville, began spelling his name with only one "s" after his grandson's meteoric rise to stardom. He died during the early 1970s and was buried in Louisville Memorial Gardens West.

Tobby Riggs, the dealer who sold the car to Presley, is also deceased. But his son Toby, who now owns Riggs Motors Inc. at 3317 Taylor Blvd., said he is certain that Burney's '57 Ford is the car that Elvis bought from his father in late November 1956.

"Believe me, it's legit," Riggs said. "I was not there at the time of the sale, but my father told me about it.

"Elvis was in town and was going to perform, and they were evidently driving down Broadway, and he glanced over, I assume, and saw this car and liked the color. Then my father got a phone call, or the company did, asking about the car.

"Who comes over but (Elvis') agent, Col. Tom Parker. As I recall there wasn't any dickering on the price. He just cut the check and that was it. That was probably the easiest sale that my father ever had. The check was signed by Parker, and I have seen a copy of the check, but I have no idea what happened to it."

Ten years ago, after an article about the car appeared in the Neighborhoods section of The Courier-Journal, Jack Fuller of Valley Station was one of several who contacted Burney with memories of the car and the Presleys.

Fuller had lived in their neighborhood and said he was among the onlookers when the car was delivered. He recalled seeing Elvis leave in the back of a pink Cadillac "with pillows all around him" and two husky bodyguards in the front seat.

Burney is a member of the Kyana Antique Automobile Club and hopes to have the '57 Ford ready for shows by early next year.

"I don't know what the car is worth," he said. "But I've had a million dollars' worth of fun out of it."

A few years before Parker died, Burney wrote the famous manager a letter inquiring about the car, but the letter came back unopened.

"It's stamped 'Return to Sender.'"

Elvis Sound Man

March 24, 1993

BILL Porter will forever be known as "Elvis Presley's sound man." Never mind that he engineered and produced 37 gold records, including some of the Everly Brothers' and Roy Orbison's biggest hits; that he is among such legendary soundsters as Les Paul, Quincy Jones and Ray Dolby in the Mix Magazine Hall of Fame; or that he founded a recording engineering program for the University of Miami at Coral Gables and taught at the University of Colorado at Denver. Above all, he is – and always will be – "Elvis Presley's sound man."

The distinction is one that the 61-year-old president of Louisville's Allen-Martin Productions accepts willingly. His collection of gold records is a virtual Fort Knox of Presley hits – "Return To Sender," "It's Now Or Never," "Surrender," "Little Sister," "Suspicious Minds," "Are You Lonesome Tonight?" and more than 20 others.

If the list is beginning to sound like one of TV's "1-800-SUPER-HITS-NOT-SOLD-IN-STORES" record offers, consider the quality and quantity of Porter's repertoire – from Roy Orbison's "Pretty Woman," "Only The Lonely" and "Crying," to Floyd Cramer's "Last Date" and Jim Reeves' "He'll Have To Go" – 579 charted records in all.

"Orbison was fantastic to work with ... but 'Only The Lonely' threw me a curve," Porter recalled. "He wanted to do this real soft voice sound of the background group singing – 'Dum-dum-dum-dumbee-doo-wah-hh' – and if you have a real soft sound in a room, you have to open the mic

Volume 3 of Elvis Presley's Greatest Hits is one of 37 gold records Bill Porter helped create.

up to hear it, then everything else pours in. You couldn't isolate things back then, so I did a whole lot of head-scratching to figure that one out. I basically wound up mixing it backwards."

In a world where acclaim usually snubs technicians and flatters entertainers, Porter turned the tables in 1960, when 15 of his records made Billboard magazine's Top 100, all in the same week.

Young Elvis Presley, fresh out of the Army, was at RCA records in Nashville that year with Porter, a young sound engineer still in his 20s who, not many years earlier, had been cruising around Nashville on a motor bike with a large transistor radio strapped to the handle bars. Porter got his start at WLAC-TV, then persuaded Chet Atkins to give him a job at RCA Records, where Porter credits Atkins with helping him learn the ropes. He next moved to Columbia Records, then to Monument Records, then to Las Vegas, where he opened his own recording studio in 1966.

In 1969, Presley asked him to help engineer the live sound for the Elvis stage show in Las Vegas. "I said, 'I don't know anything about live sound ... but I'll try,'" Porter said. "The only way I knew to do it was to mix it just like the record, because I had no other experience. I remember Sammy Davis Jr. and Gary Cooper, the movie star, going backstage and telling Elvis, 'It sounds just like your records out there.' Elvis got excited about that and said, 'Bill, you've got a steady gig.'"

Porter stayed with Presley until the singer's death.

"Elvis was a troubled man. I saw his interaction with people after his divorce from Priscilla. It hurt him pretty much," Porter said. "He was a giving sort of guy … demanding, but not unreasonable. After Elvis hired me, it's amazing how smart everybody thought I got."

Nowadays, Porter often makes personal appearances in which he discusses his memories of famous entertainers, with original music and video highlights of some of his studio work.

He still has two rings and an ID bracelet that were gifts from Presley, an uncanceled check for $109 that Presley made out to him on July 4, 1976, and the hand-held microphone that Elvis used in concert – when Bill Porter was his sound man.

In The Army With Elvis

October 7, 1988

M ACKVILLE, Ky. – If he had it to do over, DeVon Lester, 53, of Washington County, says he'd try to get to know Elvis Presley a little better.

In early 1958, Lester and Presley were drafted into the Army about the same time and wound up in the same 3rd Armored Division outfit during basic training at Fort Hood, Texas. They spent the rest of their two-year hitch at an Army post in Friedberg, West Germany. "He was just a nice guy," Lester said of Presley. "It seemed like he worked hard, and I'd say that he went through the same training the rest of us did. It seemed like he enjoyed it."

Almost as soon as Presley arrived at Fort Hood, Lester said, carloads of girls invaded the post and began circling the barracks where Presley was staying.

"I got out there and motioned to 'em that he was in our barracks," Lester said. "But it didn't work. They said, 'We know where he is.'"

Lester remembers Presley as being pretty much one of the guys, and on several occasions he recalls the legendary entertainer making casual conversation with him.

"We were mowing the yard one time, and I had a gasoline mower, and he had one of the old push-types. He said it wouldn't take very much for him to go to town and buy him a new one," Lester said.

By late 1958, Lester and Presley had been sent to West Germany, where they were assigned to the same barracks – Lester upstairs, Presley downstairs. The two were sent to Friedberg a few weeks apart, and when Lester arrived he was given Presley's slot as a tank gunner. Presley was reassigned as a jeep driver.

Although Presley actually lived off post, he arrived at the barracks early every morning, ate breakfast at the mess hall with other members of his unit, spent the day at work on the post, and was in and out of the barracks often.

"One day he came upstairs, and I think I was the only one up there," Lester recalled. "He said that he was really making the money. He said, 'I'm paying $750 house rent, and I'm making $92 a month.'"

It is doubtful that Presley was having much trouble paying the bills. "Don't Be Cruel," "All Shook Up," and several other of his early chart-busters had already vaulted him to stardom. He had appeared several times on network television in the United States; had recently starred in the films "King Creole" and "Love Me Tender," and had bought his mother a pink Cadillac.

PHOTO FROM LESTER'S COLLECTION

Elvis with Lester, June 1958.

"Two or three of the boys that had wives, but didn't have the money to bring them over (to Germany), Elvis would give them the money," Lester said.

Lester also remembers that the two floors of his barracks took turns, a week at a time, cleaning the bathrooms in the building. Presley, he said, paid an outside custodial service to clean the bathrooms for the men on his floor.

"He seemed like one of the nicest boys we had, and I believe everybody thought a lot of him," Lester said. "Of course we all wore name tags, and whenever he'd meet you, more than likely he'd call you by your last name. They said he didn't smoke or drink, but I saw him with a cigar two or three times."

Lester said he doesn't recall that Presley partied much with the other soldiers, and he said the singer once told them that, because of his recording contract with RCA, he could not give a private concert for his Army buddies.

PHOTO BY BYRON CRAWFORD

"Some of my girlfriends over there, you wouldn't believe this, but they were going with me, trying to get me to get them dates with Elvis," Lester said. "That didn't go over very good."

In early 1960, Lester and Presley, both 25, were discharged from the Army. Presley had attained the rank of sergeant, and Lester was a private first class.

Presley continued his show business career, appearing on the "Frank Sinatra – Timex Special" a few weeks later, then starring in a string of successful motion pictures, including "G.I. Blues," "Flaming Star" and "Blue Hawaii."

Lester went back to milking cows and raising tobacco in Central Kentucky, and later married Patsy Russell, a school counselor at Mackville. He still farms, but also works as a utility man at Mercer County High School in Harrodsburg. He doesn't believe the recent rash of tales that Presley, who died in August 1977, is still alive. For several years after Lester returned to Kentucky, there were rumors – all untrue – that Presley visited him.

"I guess the last time I saw him was in the mess hall," Lester said.

Club 68 and Club Cherry

September 8, 1995

L EBANON, Ky. – If Hyleme George and Obie Slater wanted to, they could fill a wing at Cleveland's new Rock and Roll Hall of Fame with their recollections of legendary rockers.

Back in the 1960s, when George owned Lebanon's Club 68 and the Club Cherry a few blocks away, he and Slater, who managed the Club Cherry and handled all the bookings, brushed shoulders with many of those now enshrined in the hall. Although George and Slater have forgotten several names, they reminisced recently and counted 86 famous bands or entertainers who passed through the doors of the two Marion County clubs during their heyday.

The Club 68, which catered to a predominantly white clientele, opened in 1964 with Lloyd Price of "Stagger Lee" fame. Nat King Cole, Ike and Tina Turner, the Kingsmen, Sir Douglas Quintet, Jerry Lee Lewis, Rufus Thomas, Credence Clearwater Revival, The Tommy Dorsey Orchestra, Steppenwolf, the Platters, the Amazing Rhythm Aces and many other stars played there.

But it was the Club Cherry, a nightspot for African Americans, on Water Street in Lebanon, that was to become the most popular stopover for dozens of musicians en route to the Hall of Fame.

Obie Slater remembers Otis Redding, Jimi Hendrix, Little Richard, Clyde McPhatter, Bo Diddley, Jackie Wilson, the Supremes, James Brown, Ray Charles, Fats Domino and Chuck Berry. He can tell you stories about Ike and Tina Turner, Sam and Dave, Wilson Pickett, B.B.

199

PHOTO BY BYRON CRAWFORD

Hyleme George, left, and Obie Slater stood outside the old Club 68 building in Lebanon. In the 1960s, George owned Club 68 and the Club Cherry, a few blocks away, which Slater managed.

King, Percy Sledge, Eddie Floyd, Hank Ballard and the Midnighters. He also tells stories about Junior Parker, Joe Tex, Laverne Baker, the Coasters, the Shirelles, Bobby Blue Bland and more than 30 other big-name rock, blues and jazz entertainers, including Dinah Washington and Count Basie, who appeared at the Club Cherry.

"The night Count Basie was there, my audience was all white," Slater said. "The first time I had Otis Redding, I got him and his band for three nights for $500. Jimi Hendrix played for me when he was nobody.

He was a beautiful person. He played guitar behind his head, played it with his teeth, with his toes. Plus, he was a pretty good little singer then. A fella called Johnny Jones, a house painter, taught him how to play. I assume Johnny Jones is still painting." Then there was Little Richard, who George and Slater say titled his song "Lucille" after the girlfriend of a former manager of the Club Cherry.

Things did not always go smoothly at the clubs in Lebanon when big-name talent was in town. Slater recalls that Otis Redding hit one of his band members in the mouth one night for missing one note during a song.

"He said, 'Don't mess up my music,'" Slater said. "James Brown cut one of his fellas for missing a note. James was a pain. He was a mean little rascal."

Slater lost $1,500 when he booked the great Jackie Wilson and the crowd he expected didn't show. When his banker asked what was wrong a few days later, Slater used Wilson's smash hit single to answer – "Jackie Wilson left me with 'Lonely Teardrops.'"

Slater, 66, who now operates Obie's Record Shop in Danville, and George, 83, a former mayor of Lebanon who is retired and still lives there, can regale listeners for hours with stories from the other side of rock 'n' roll.

Hyleme George recalls that Nat King Cole came to the Club 68 for $500; that the Kingsmen, of "Louie Louie" fame, came for $750; and that 1,500 people showed up. He remembers when he had to lend Ike and Tina money for gas.

And he remembers that when he booked Jerry Lee Lewis at the Club 68, the singer arrived in pajamas and, in George's words, "about four-fifths drunk."

The original Club 68 sign invites folks to come in for some "Rock-n-Roll."

PHOTO COURTESY OF JOEY GEORGE, SON OF ELMER GEORGE

Despite an earlier contract agreement, George said, Lewis tried to double his price after the concert had sold out. When George refused to pay, word came that "Jerry Lee's not going to play."

Then word reached Lewis that maybe he wouldn't play in Lebanon, or anywhere else, if he happened to get all his fingers broken before he left town. Those who were at his concert that night said "The Killer" played "Great Balls of Fire" as it had never been played before.

The Club Cherry burned many years ago, and the Club 68 closed several years back. Someone stole all of Obie Slater's pictures, and Hyleme George never kept any of his contracts with famous rockers. But they sure can tell some stories.

Footnote: The original "Club 68" sign has now been moved to the home of Lebanon attorney Elmer George, a nephew of Hyleme, who owns the former club property. After Hyleme's death, Obie Slater lived in a home on the property owned by Hyleme's great-nephew, Dallas George.

Doo-Wop Encore

July 17, 2005

LET'S hear it one more time for Paul Penny, the Carnations and Tren-Dells!
Forty-four years ago this summer, as a teenager roaming the Kentucky State Fair, I remember peeping wide-eyed through a locked gate at Fairgrounds Stadium while singer Bobby Vee was rehearsing for a concert that night.

It was his backup vocal group, the locally popular Tren-Dells, that held me spellbound with their smooth, "woooooos" on Bobby Vee's "Take Good Care of My Baby."

"Gosh!" I thought. "This sounds even better than the song sounds on the old car radio!"

One of the voices of the Tren-Dells that day was Paul Penny, who has remained in Louisville and is still singing at age 63. Last week I finally got a chance to shake his hand and tell him how much I had enjoyed the Tren-Dells' rehearsal that summer afternoon long ago, and that I still had a record album, titled "Fourteen By Request," featuring many of the great Louisville bands of the 1960s.

It includes the Tren-Dells and Carnations, vocal and instrumental groups that worked together, along with Penny, who, besides being a solo vocalist, plays drums, guitar and piano, and performed with the Carnations and Tren-Dells during their heyday.

"Along the way we worked with some big artists like Bobby Vee, Bo

Diddley and the Dick Clark Caravan of Stars," said Penny. "When Buddy Holly, Ritchie Valens and The Big Bopper got killed on the airplane, they were scheduled to be at Memorial Auditorium (in Louisville) on a certain date, and we were going to be there with them."

During the conversation, the two of us got lost in the 1950s and 1960s, recalling some of the other early groups whose music helped define a decade in Louisville. There were Cosmo & the Counts, Janie Moss and the Epics, The Sultans, the still-great Monarchs and many others.

Penny, whose real name is Paul Stodghill, dug out a CD titled "Louisville's Original Hit Makers" that features, among songs from some other groups, his "I'm So Young" with the Tren-Dells, Johnny Hourigan and the Tren-Dells' "Moments Like This," "Nite Owl" and others.

Hardy Martin and the Carnations' "Scorpion" featured Penny on drums, and he played piano on the Monarchs' hit "This Old Heart."

PHOTO COURTESY OF PAUL PENNY

The Carnations, Tren-Dells and Paul Penny about circa 1959, includes from left, Tommy Summitt and Bill Summitt of the Tren-Dells, kneeling. Ray Allen of the Carnations, standing, and Carnations Hardy Martin, with guitar, Duke Marsh with sax, Ronnie Lloyd on drums and Vernon Felty with guitar. Paul Penny is standing far right, and Tren-Dells Johnny Hourigan, smiling, and Bill Mathley are kneeling far right.

Promotion of their music by early WAKY Radio deejays Al Dun-
away and Jack Sanders helped make stars of many of the local groups.
Although the Carnations, Tren-Dells and most others would not survive
much beyond the 1960s, some of the band members, such as Hardy Martin and Ray Allen of the Carnations, would go on to success in the audio/
video production industry.

Tommy Thomas, assistant manager of a record store in Louisville's
Summit, said there is still an interest in the work of popular local groups
of the 1960s, mostly among baby boomers who once had the groups'
work in their record collection and want it back, and occasionally among
younger people who have come to appreciate the music.

A while back, when Penny was performing at the Moose Lodge on
Fegenbush Lane, he said brothers Tommy and Bill Summitt, two original
Tren-Dells, showed up in the audience and he persuaded them to sing
with him. Duke Marsh, one of the original Carnations, was playing key-
board and sax that night. One thing led to another, and the guys decided
to get together all the former Carnations and Tren-Dells they could find
for a one-night reunion.

They booked the music hall at Scottsburg, Indiana, for July 23rd.

I told Penny I'd be there when the doors open if I could scrounge up
the $10 admission. If not I'd be standing just outside, peeping through a
crack in the door, and remembering a summer afternoon at the Kentucky
State Fair 44 years ago.

"You Belong To Me"

January 3, 2001

"See the pyramids along the Nile,
Watch the sunrise from a tropic isle,
Just remember, darling, all the while,
You belong to me..."

MOST baby boomers can hum the melody to "You Belong to Me," and many remember the lyrics to the golden oldie. Chilton Searcy Price of Louisville, who wrote the words and music in the early 1950s, sat at the grand piano in her living room recently and played it one more time, just for me.

She would not attempt to sing it, Price said apologetically, because she did not like the way she sounds at age 87. But as soon as she began to play and I noticed that her eyes were closed, I knew this performance would be among my memories' best.

I heard Jo Stafford's original recording that went to No. 1 on the Hit Parade in the early 1950s. And in the summer of 1962, I was a teenager when a remake by a doo-wop group called the Duprees stayed on Billboard's Top 10 for more than two months. But hearing and watching Price play it now, between the sunset of one millennium and the dawn of another, was as good as it gets.

After she finished an encore, Price showed me the gold record she got from Columbia Records when "You Belong to Me" sold over one million copies, a date she has long since forgotten.

It was her second gold record. The first was "Slow Poke," which was recorded exactly as she wrote it by the late Pee Wee King of Louisville, and which has now sold over two million copies.

In the sheet music under the piano bench we found a few of her songs that Doris Day, Dinah Shore, Tony Bennett, Patti Page and other stars recorded. There was the sheet music from Universal Pictures' "Forbidden," starring Tony Curtis and Joanne Dru, which featured "You Belong to Me."

PHOTO BY BYRON CRAWFORD

Chilton Searcy Price

Price wrote her first song, "Making Up My Mind," at age 14 as a student at Atherton High School. Her father, Chesley Searcy, a lawyer, had taught her piano. "I hear a title, and a title usually sends me to a melody."

She played violin and studied music at the University of Louisville, and in the early 1940s was a member of the Louisville Orchestra. While working briefly as a music librarian at WAVE Radio in Louisville during the early 1950s she got acquainted with band leader King and gave him a few songs she had written.

King recorded "Slow Poke" himself and sent "You Belong to Me" to orchestra leader Mitch Miller, who first gave it to Joni James, and then to Stafford.

"After that, Mitch began to call me and ask, 'What have you got?' And I would take a tape recorder and play it over the phone for him," Price said. "He got me in with Doris Day's publisher for 'Never Look Back,' which was in one of her movies."

Price is still writing songs at her home in eastern Louisville. She writes songs now, she says, just for enjoyment and for her grandchildren. Despite the fact that her music of half a century ago is still earning royalties, she doubts that any publisher would be interested in her music today.

"Not long ago at the Boat Club they were having a 50th-anniversary party for a couple, and wanted somebody to play the piano who knew all the old stuff. They asked me, and paid me," Price said. "I played an hour and a half, and had more fun than the law allows."

Footnote: Film and recording credits for "You Belong To Me" have included but may not be limited to: Jo Stafford (1952), Sonny Till & The Orioles (1952), The Duprees (1962), Joni James, Patti Page, Johnny Mathis, Patsy Cline, Doris Day, Dean Martin, Floyd Cramer, Kathie Lee Gifford, "Mona Lisa Smile" Tori Amos (2003), "Shrek" (2001) Jason Wade, "Ally McBeal," Vonda Shepard.

Chilton Price died in January 2010 at age 96.

The Singing Hilltoppers

June 15, 2007

L ONG before Elvis or the Beatles ever played The Ed Sullivan Show, the Hilltoppers, a vocal group from Western Kentucky University, took center stage.

Their October 26, 1952, appearance on CBS Television, only six months after their first record was released, was seen by an estimated 40 million viewers.

Lead singer Jimmy Sacca and Billy Vaughn, Don McGuire and Seymour Spiegelman got acquainted at two college hangouts in Bowling Green, where Vaughn, a musician from nearby Glasgow, often performed.

Sacca, from Lockport, N.Y., was a football player at Western. McGuire, from Hazard, was a WKU basketball player. Spiegelman, from Seneca Falls, N.Y., was on a music scholarship.

The group not only borrowed Western's team nickname of Hilltoppers but dressed in red-and-gray Western beanies and red sweaters emblazoned with a large "W."

The day after the television show, their popular love ballad, "Trying," sold 100,000 copies. It already was among the top five best-sellers in New York, Chicago, Pittsburgh and New Orleans.

Their "P.S. I Love You" sold over a million copies in 1953. Their "Only You," which may have featured later members of the group, remained on the British charts for 26 weeks.

Sacca reflected that fate seemed to have brought the group together.
"How else can you explain how a kid like me ... could find his way to
Western Kentucky, meet three other guys and end up on The Ed Sullivan
Show, almost overnight?" he said.

Their first hit was recorded on a $30 reel-to-reel tape machine while
one of their buddies, Bill "Greek" Ploumis, lay with his head on a book
to hold down the broken soft pedal on the piano, their only accompani-
ment on the stage of the empty auditorium at what then was Western
Kentucky State College.

Now, 55 years later, Western Kentucky University history professor
Carlton Jackson has written the story of the group's phenomenal rise to
stardom in "P.S. I Love You, The story of the Singing Hilltoppers" (The
University Press of Kentucky).

Jackson's conversations
in the mid-1980s with
Vaughn, who became a
prominent orchestra leader
and recording artist on his
own, set the stage for the
book.

Noted Kentucky author
Bobbie Ann Mason, the
first national president of
the Hilltoppers Fan Club,
also helped with research,
along with the two sur-
viving original members
of the group, Sacca and
McGuire, who both live in
Lexington.

"They gave the world
a kind of music that, as
McGuire explained, 'didn't
abuse anyone's ears,'" said
Jackson.

After The Ed Sul-
livan Show, life for the

PHOTO COURTESY OF THE UNIVERSITY PRESS OF KENTUCKY

*Members of the Hilltoppers include: Jimmy
Sacca (top), Billy Vaughn (in beanie), Don
McGuire (bottom), and Seymour Spiegelman
(far right).*

Hilltoppers was juggled between classes and concerts. They drove a Cadillac Fleetwood or traveled by plane, their songs were on the radio, and coeds swooned when they stepped on stage.

There were network TV appearances on American Bandstand, The Today Show, and The Steve Allen Show. They were voted Cashbox magazine's Top Vocal Group of 1953.

But the military draft, the emergence of rock 'n' roll, marriage, families and the rigors of life on the road finally brought the Hilltoppers back down to earth.

Although they enjoyed several more years of popularity, even with different singers, they never regained the prominence they had known in 1952 and '53. You can read all about it in Jackson's book, and you can see an extensive Hilltoppers memorabilia collection, including Mason's mementos, at the Kentucky Museum at Western Kentucky University.

Flowers For Secretariat

May 6, 2005

PARIS, Ky. – I should have left a rose at the grave of Secretariat. Many Claiborne Farm visitors do.

"Within the next week, he'll have close to 80 to 100 roses - and these are real, not artificial," said Claiborne stallion foreman Jim Zajic. "Secretariat's the one that gets the flowers and mints."

The horse cemetery at Claiborne Farm near Paris - where the big chestnut Triple Crown winner spent most of his life and died in 1989 - is a virtual thoroughbred hall of fame.

It is lined with the stone markers of such legendary horses as Secretariat's father and grandfather – Bold Ruler and Nasrullah. Also there are: Gallant Fox; Round Table; Blenheim II, who sired Whirlaway and Jet Pilot; Johnstown; Buckpasser; Nijinski II; Riva Ridge; Sir Gallahad III; Swale; Hoist the Flag; Mr. Prospector; and others.

Yet, it is Secretariat, the 1973 Triple Crown winner, whose grave is always sprinkled with mints and flowers.

"Red and white starlight mints are very popular with the stallions now, so the grooms give them the mints when they want them to come to the gate. People sometimes bring them and leave them at the grave," Zajic said. "One couple brings a basket of flowers in March on Secretariat's birthday, and there's also some people who send a fresh bouquet of mums in October when the 'big horse' passed away."

How did Secretariat so completely capture the hearts of race fans and horse-lovers across America?

Some say it was because he came along at a time when the nation was looking for a way to help heal the deep scars of the Vietnam War. Others believe it was Secretariat's good looks, talent and personality.

Claiborne Farm manager Gus Koch probably summed it up best: "He had charisma. He was a champion and he knew it. He liked people and liked having his picture made. And he was so smart that you almost got the feeling he could load film into people's cameras."

Secretariat's grave at Claiborne Farm near Paris is always sprinkled with peppermints and flowers.

PHOTO BY BYRON CRAWFORD

My most vivid memory of Secretariat is of seeing him shift into passing gear down the stretch of the 1973 Derby to cross the finish line in record time, just below where I was standing on a roof adjacent to the press box, in the shadow of the twin spires.

I think I realized in that moment that - for me, as far as race horses and Derbys went - it couldn't get much better than that, and it never has.

Secretariat would go on to win the Triple Crown and forever become, to countless millions of us, what the great Man O' War was to fans of another era: "The mostest hoss," as he was often described by his famous groom and best friend, Will Harbut.

"We can produce horses for the rest of our lives, but for the public there'll never be another Secretariat," Zajic said. "And for people who race horses – when you lead a horse onto the track, and every time he performs, he's close to a track record with some of the greatest horses that ever raced - it's a tough chore to get another one like him."

He was so good that even now, Secretariat still wins the run for the roses during Derby week, among all those other famous thoroughbreds in the horse cemetery at Claiborne Farm.

Buddha of Ballistics ...
and Wit

April 19, 1995

BROOKLYN, Ky. – "It is the only cave in Kentucky where Daniel Boone never spent the winter," Col. George Chinn used to joke of the cavern he hollowed out in the limestone palisades near his Mercer County home on the Kentucky River.

Chinn, a Marine Corps colonel who was a weapons troubleshooter in World War II and Korea, then was called back into the corps at age 64 for service during the Vietnam War, would be on the short list of the most unforgettable characters I have met.

Although he died in 1987 at age 85, there is rarely a discussion of Kentucky history, politics, Kentucky River folk life, military machine guns or the legendary 1921 Centre-Harvard football game in which his name doesn't come up.

All his life, George Chinn seemed either to sail along in history's wake or help create it.

He was a member of that Centre College team that beat Harvard 6-0 in what some sportswriters have called the game of the century. His family had the 1883 Kentucky Derby winner, Leonatus. His grandfather was walking beside Gov. William Goebel when Goebel was assassinated.

Chinn wrote several books of history and was director of the Kentucky Historical Society. He was among the nation's leading authorities

213

on automatic weapons, held several weapon patents and wrote
"The Machine Gun," the Navy's
five volume reference work on
the subject. One magazine writer
called him "the Buddha of Bal-
listics," And Encyclopedia Bri-
tannica asked him to author its
machine-gun section.

Yet among those who knew
him best, his most endearing
qualities were his humility, common sense and inimitable wit. His
grandson, Howard "Buddy" Howells II of Harrodsburg, remembers
the colonel telling him that when talking pictures came to movie houses,
the Western gunfights he watched from the front row were so realistic
that he often suffered powder burns.

Chinn's storied Cave House was inspired by his visit to North Carolina's Bat Cave while he was a young man. In the late 1920's, using blasting
techniques he had learned at his grandfather's fluorspar mine along the
Kentucky River, Chinn blew out a tunnel a few hundred feet long into
the side of a cliff beside U.S. 68 just west of Brooklyn Bridge, and started
what he later called a speakeasy.

Passers-by were lured into the cave with inexpensive ham sandwiches
and foot-long hot dogs, but the profits were from a bar and slot machines.
When Chinn was finally hauled into court for running an illegal game of
chance, the story goes, he successfully defended himself by proving that
he had rigged the machines to eliminate chance, any chance of winning.

The Cave House was finally closed in the late 1930's, but years later it
was reopened and fitted with some armor plating after Col. Chinn was
called back into service to develop a gun that could be used against snip-
ers in the jungles of Vietnam.

Within seven-and-a-half months, Chinn, with the help of a handful of other experts and the Naval Ordnance Station in Louisville, had
produced the Mk-19 high-velocity grenade launcher. In 60 seconds this
46-pound weapon could drop 300 pounds of explosives on small targets

1.5 miles away. The gun was used successfully in Vietnam and more re-cently in the Persian Gulf War. Chinn also headed development of the Mk-22, 20/30 mm cannon, using the cave as a firing range.

Given the colonel's penchant for humor, it should have come as no surprise that one day, just after a heavy barrage of firing, an attractive, well-dressed woman stepped through the doorway of the Cave House into the haze of gun smoke.

"Excuse me," she said to Col. Chinn, "Do you still serve ham sand-wiches here?"

"Yes, ma'am," the colonel politely replied, "but we've just finished shooting the hogs, and it'll be a while."

David Dick

November 10, 1995

LUM LICK, Ky. – David Dick is proving that you *can* go home again, or at least get awfully close.

The Emmy-award-winning former CBS News correspondent, who grew up in rural Bourbon County, has found peace, fulfillment and room to write in his ancestral farm home on the waters of Plum Lick Creek.

He has left the jets on which he circled the globe for a dilapidated farm pickup named "Ole Blue." He has swapped his microphone and a spot on the CBS Evening News for a flock of sheep and a herd of cattle. He has given up rooms in exotic hotels for a 214-acre farm and an 1850s farmhouse that got city water only a few weeks ago. And he has turned his back on the bright lights of network television for the glow of a fireplace and the warm hugs of his wife, Lalie, a former executive for Revlon International, and their 12-year-old daughter, Ravy. (He also has four grown children from a previous marriage.)

After 19 years of covering presidential campaigns, wars in Central America and the Middle East, and the mass suicide of more than 900 people at Jonestown, Guyana, he is now a farmer who moonlights as a writer and journalism professor at the University of Kentucky.

Settled in with a cup of hot cider, beside a crackling fire where he can peep out the window at the chilly sunset in the rolling hills beyond Plum Lick, the 65-year-old journalist is on the phone with Carl West of the

Frankfort State Journal. West, who runs the Kentucky Book Fair, says he has just gotten a call from Andy Rooney of CBS' "60 Minutes," who said he will be in Frankfort for the Nov. 18 book fair.

"I had made a call to Andy some time ago - really, I hardly knew him at all - and told him about the book fair," Dick chuckled as he hung up the phone. "He said to have them write him, and they did, but he never answered. Then, 10 minutes ago, he called Carl and said he'd be there."

Dick will be there, too. He has made a splendid transition from broadcast to print since his departure from the network in 1985. His homespun "The View from Plum Lick," back-page essays in *Kentucky Living* magazine, has endeared him to a wide and admiring audience around the state and has opened the door for his growing success as an author.

He now has four books to his credit - "Peace at the Center," "The View From Plum Lick," "Follow The Storm" and "A Conversation With Peter P. Pence" - which he will sign at Nature's Crossing in Middletown from 10 a.m. to 3 p.m. tomorrow.

The son of a doctor, Dick was born in Cincinnati but moved to Kentucky with his mother after his father died when David was 18 months old. He worked on the farm, but he was "not a good cowboy."

"I was not good with my hands," he said. "I was romantic. I always knew I wanted to write, but I was not precocious. I scribbled some things, and tried my hand at verse.... When I got through high school, I took a trip to Mexico and wrote about it, and got paid a penny a word from some youth magazine. That was my publishing debut."

It was to be the first of many journeys and stories for Dick, who attended UK for a while, then joined the Navy, worked with the Armed

Forces Radio and Television Service in the Philippines, then returned to UK. He earned a master's degree in English, got fired from WVLK radio, then got a job at WHAS radio and TV in Louisville in 1959 and was hired by CBS seven years later.

"It was exciting, supercharged, irreverent, crazy. Right out on the cutting edge," he said of the network job. "I guess until I got on the presidential campaigns ... I didn't know what it felt like to have adrenaline pumping. But when I got a taste of it, I couldn't hardly get off that high. I don't use that as an excuse for why my first marriage of 25 years came to an end, but it did.

"I remind students all the time, 'If you want to work for the network - it's not conventional (work), it's not normal.'"

Through it all, Dick found secret refuge in his memories of "a piece of green" cradled in the hills of his Kentucky homeland, on a little creek called Plum Lick. And when at last he had had enough of jets, bright lights and deadlines, he returned from all over the world to share the peace of Plum Lick as only he could describe it: the peace of being home from everywhere.

Thanks, Carl

November 12, 2006

K ENTUCKY owes Carl West a "thank you" note for not sending the books back.

Twenty five years ago, when he founded the Kentucky Book Fair, the brusque editor of The State Journal in Frankfort, a former Washington correspondent for Scripps-Howard Newspapers, insisted to his many doubters that the fair could be a successful long-term event.

West had been library chairman of the National Press Club, where he successfully organized a book fair to raise library funds. His hope for the Kentucky event was to bring together books, readers and authors, mainly from Kentucky, for a day of buying and selling, autographing and in-person chats.

The book fair's modest share of the proceeds would be passed along to struggling libraries across the state. Almost until the doors opened on that rainy Saturday of the first fair, some of West's trusted friends were still urging that he cancel the event and send the books back.

"They were thinking there weren't as many readers in Kentucky as there were elsewhere," said West. Well, there were enough to build the Kentucky Book Fair into an immensely popular regional event that now draws as many as 5,000 book lovers and more than 200 authors to Frankfort's Convention Center.

This year, more than 300 authors were turned away. Book sales at the fair have totaled about 2.5 million and gifts to Kentucky's libraries and literacy programs are nearing $300,000.

In addition to Kentucky authors Wendell Berry, Bobbie Ann Mason, Frank X. Walker, David Dick, Silas House and countless others, the Kentucky Book Fair's list of visiting celebrity authors has spanned a wide range of personalities, from Erma Bombeck, Andy Rooney, Mickey Mantle and Olympian Carl Lewis, to former first lady Rosalynn Carter and Pulitzer Prize winners David Halberstam and Harrison Salisbury, to this year's guest, Oscar-winning actress Patricia Neal.

Carl West

Neal, a native of southeastern Kentucky, signed her biography, "Patricia Neal: An Unquiet Life."

"Carl West is the absolute backbone of this," said Lynda Sherrard, a veteran board member and the chairwoman of the 25th Kentucky Book Fair. "He always steps back and tries to avoid taking credit, but the truth is he's the driving force. When we try to get more frivolous, or try to make it more than a book fair with other things, he always draws us back to our central course."

The late John Ed Pearce, a master wordsmith, could forge no better phrase than "stubborn determination" in characterizing West's unwavering leadership.

A special table at yesterday's Kentucky Book Fair featured the books of one of the fair's most revered authors, the late Kentucky historian Dr. Thomas Clark, who died in 2005 near the age of 102.

West credits Clark as being "the unseen hand" that guided the book fair, and insists that the fair's many volunteers are the true secret of its success. Clark, however, wrote a "thank you" note to Carl West every year. In December 1999, he wrote: "I must stop my conscience from hurting me before this year, this century and this millennium end. I am most appreciative to the Kentucky Book Fair. To me, this is one of the truly good things to come out of the 20th Century."

Well said – P.S., Carl, thanks for not sending the books back.

Allen Purnell

March 11, 2005

S IMPSONVILLE, Ky. – The sausage king who cooked up a successful, long-term marketing campaign with little more than a big
smile and the words, "It's goooood!" still doesn't have a computer
in his office.

"I just didn't want to fool with it," said Allen Purnell, chairman of the
board of Purnell's Old Folks Country Sausage. "Everybody that's supposed to know something around here uses one, but the only thing I've
got on my desk is an adding machine."

When Purnell graduated in 1954 from Louisville's Atherton High
School, where he was a city all-star football tackle, his yearbook prophecy
said that he would become a "salesman."

He is that, to be sure. The Tennessee drawl that he brought from
Nashville when his parents, F.B. and Clara Purnell, their three sons and
a daughter moved to Louisville in 1950 would serve Allen well when he
took to the road selling his family's sausage after graduation.

A mouth-watering, now-secret recipe that his grandmother used on
the farm in Tennessee has helped, too.

F. B. Purnell worked for the Nashville, Chattanooga and St. Louis
Railroad in those days, but often took his homemade sausage and biscuits
to work for lunch, and sometimes shared them with other railroaders.
Soon, F.B. was taking orders for his next batch of sausage.

When he began selling to small groceries around Middle Tennessee, he gave the sausage his nick-name, "Old Folks," which he had picked up from a favorite childhood pastime of listening to old folks tell stories.

The Purnells moved to Louisville after a spice salesman convinced F.B. Purnell there wasn't any good sausage in Louisville and there would be a strong market for his products in Kentucky. By 1955 the family had relocated to Shelby County and built a plant in Simpsonville.

Allen married Ann Miller, a high school typing teacher, and the couple raised four children on their farm near Simpson-ville. Allen's brother, Bob, is now secretary-treasurer of the company; Allen's son, Todd, is president; and Mike, son of Fred, Allen and Bob's late brother, is the parts buyer.

The family also owns the historic Old Stone Inn restaurant adjacent to the F.B. Purnell Sausage Co. The company employs about 300 people and has customers in 44 states.

A recent issue of Meat Marketing & Technology magazine lists Purnell's sausage among the top 10 in the United States in retail sales.

Veteran retail sales manager Bob Sutherland said Purnell's homegrown image is the real thing, not a phony advertising gimmick.

"I don't hardly know how we could hide it," Sutherland insists.

Allen Purnell's folksy, "It's goooood!" radio commercials that began during University of Kentucky football and basketball broadcasts in the 1960's eventually expanded to Nashville's Grand Ole Opry, and are on telecasts of Southeastern Conference games.

"Daddy had 'It's good' on his first package," Allen Purnell said, "and I just drug it out a little bit, and it took hold."

Newsreel
Rosie-the-Riveter

June 2, 2002

W**HEN** Sotheby's in New York auctioned Norman Rockwell's well-known "Rosie the Riveter" painting for $4.5 million a few days ago, Connie Gibson and Vickie Jarvis, both of Clarksville, Ind., must have smiled and imagined what their late mother would have said about the price.

Their mother, Rose Will Monroe, a native of Science Hill in Pulaski County, was the real World War II-era Rosie the Riveter to many movie-going Americans of that day. She died in Clarksville in 1997 at the age of 77.

Rose Monroe was not the model for Rockwell's famous painting - or for any of the other Rosie the Riveter wartime posters that encouraged American women to work in factories on the home front while men were away at war. But she became the motion picture version of Rosie the Riveter in the early 1940s while working as a riveter in an aircraft plant that made B-24s and B-29s in Ypsilanti, Mich.

The song "Rosie the Riveter" was popular when a film crew was visiting the factory with actor Walter Pidgeon producing a movie newsreel to sell war bonds. When Monroe's foreman told the filmmakers there was a real Rosie the Riveter working at the plant, a Central Kentucky farm girl armed with a rivet gun suddenly became the silver screen's real-life Rosie.

"It was a case of her being at the right place at the right time," said Jarvis, 48. "Mom never really made anything of this or pushed it at all, and never ever said to anyone that those posters were pictures of her, nor have we."

Gibson, 64, said her mother had seen the newsreel in which she was featured at a theater when it was released, and again years later when she was honored by a Business and Professional Women's Club. But her mother never got a copy of the film and her daughters have never seen it.

"Mom never realized much of the fame, as such," Gibson said. "It really wasn't picked up on until her funeral, when it was included in her obituary about her being a Rosie the Riveter. That's where the fame started pretty much, then."

The sisters recalled that their mother was the lifelong personification of the Rosie the Riveter "We can do it" spirit.

FAMILY PHOTO

Monroe, a mother of three, also worked as a taxi driver; at the old Curtiss-Wright factory and as a homebuilder in Southern Indiana. She died in 1997 at the age of 77. Rose Monroe was not the model for any of the well-known Rosie the Riveter wartime posters. But she became the motion picture version of Rosie in the early 1940s while working as a riveter in an aircraft plant in Ypsilanti, Mich.

"Mom taught us by her actions that there was nothing we couldn't do if we set our minds to it," Gibson said. "She didn't believe gender should play a part if you were qualified, and she always said, 'Don't ask someone else to do for you what you can do for yourself.' She was an extremely hard worker, but was very funny, loved to have a good time and was an outdoors person."

Monroe wanted to work as a ferry pilot for military aircraft - delivering newly built planes from factories to deployment sites, as some women pilots did in the war years. But she had been turned down for pilot training because she had two young children at the time. Yet the desire to fly never left her, and in the early 1970s, she got her pilot's license.

She once worked as a taxi driver in Louisville, and at the old Curtiss-Wright factory on the outskirts of the city. She walked several miles after getting off work at the factory to attend beauty school. Later in life she became a home builder in Southern Indiana.

She lost one of her three children, a son, many years ago. Today, her daughter Vickie is a licensed pilot and skydiving instructor. Connie retired after running her own wallpaper business. The American Battle Monument Commission created the Rose Monroe Society Fund a few years ago as part of its drive to raise money for the World War II Memorial.

PART FOUR:

Reflections,
Mementoes & Regrets

Love on the Beech

May 29, 1994

BUTLER, Ky. — On a wooded bluff above the Licking River in Campbell County there stands a scarred old beech tree. On its trunk is carved a faded heart with an arrow and three sets of initials: S.S., E.V. and then J.F. squeezed in at the bottom.

Frank Florence Jr., 72, and his wife Betty, 68, were 17 and 13 when the heart was carved. At the time, Frank's father owned the farm where the tree stood. A neighbor boy whose initials were S.S. carved the heart and his initials with those of Elizabeth "Betty" Vater, the girl on whom both he and Frank had a crush.

Frank saw the carving and tried to scratch out the other boy's initials, then added his own, J.F. (Junior Florence), in smaller letters at the bottom. So began his quest for a place in the heart of the woman who now has been his wife for 51 years.

"She was really, really pretty, and she was vivacious," Frank said. "Most of the boys in school liked her,

229

and of the two or three girls that I thought the most of, she was number one." There were complications, however. Betty's parents didn't approve of Frank, mostly because he was older. They wanted her to date a family friend.

"As far as actual dates, we only had one, in July 1942," Frank remembered. "We went to see the movie 'Hold Back the Dawn,' with Charles Boyer and Olivia de Havilland."

The wartime melodrama would forever be their movie. Frank persuaded Betty to give him a kiss when he took her home that night.

"He really had a line," Betty said. "He had been drafted into the Army and said he was going overseas and that he might not come back, and what could one little kiss hurt? My mother happened to be looking out the window and saw it, and said 'You're not writing to him. You're not seeing him anymore, or anything.'"

Not long afterward, in January 1943, the two were married secretly in Richmond, when Betty, 17, a high school senior, visited the college there with some of her friends. Frank, 21, managed a weekend pass from an Army post in Tennessee. One of Betty's friends who was older posed as Betty and gave her age as 21 to get a marriage license.

"Moonlight Becomes You," which was No. 1 on the Hit Parade for 13 weeks that winter, became Frank and Betty's song for life.

Betty's parents did not learn until three months later that she had eloped. They threatened to have the marriage annulled, but Frank, then a machine-gunner in the Army, talked them out of it by letter.

In the fall of 1944 word came that he was missing in action in France and that his brother had been killed. Months passed with no word. Everyone except Betty gave up hope. She wrote letters every day and sent them to his last known address. Finally, after five months of waiting, she got a postcard saying he was a prisoner of war in Germany. He never got her letters until he got home. Then he read all 300 of them.

Betty later graduated from the University of Louisville and Frank from Georgetown College and the Southern Baptist Theological Seminary.

They had three children: Terry, Linda and Nancy. Betty became a teacher and he became a minister. They served as missionaries in South America for a few years.

Frank still preaches occasionally, and he writes photo captions for "Reminisce" magazine. Betty writes and makes quilts and dolls. They live in tiny Peach Grove in Pendleton County, a few miles from where their initials were left in the old beech tree.

"Moonlight Becomes You" is still their song, and although they can no longer walk to the tree above the river, they still open the family photo album to the page that holds their fading snapshots of the heart.

Summer Without T.V.

November 8, 1995

"THIS must have been written the summer we turned off the T.V.," my wife mused, handing me a letter that our son, Joe, had written at age nine to then-President Ronald Reagan. She had found the letter in a cache of scrapbook items unearthed in the catacombs of the storage room.

Vaguely, I remembered the summer she turned off the T.V. School was barely out and our four children were already becoming zombies. We would find them sprawled about the den in their pajamas all day, staring hypnotically at the screen. So one morning their mother clicked off the television and said, "That's it, the T.V. is off the rest of the summer. You're on vacation, so find something interesting to do."

Almost immediately our children were transformed into real people again. Instead of numbly reacting to the canned laughter and artificial violence on T.V., they laughed real laughs and fought real fights, with each other. They learned real lessons about real life.

We heard them talking, and saw them reading books and drawing. They banged on the old piano and sang. They found a guitar and tried to play it. They played ball with each other in the yard and ran barefoot in the dust. They chased lightning bugs, climbed trees, fished, picked wild blackberries and fed calves on the bottle. They picked apples and sold them on the roadside in front of the house.

The three younger children decided to clean out a cluttered outbuilding

232

and make themselves a playhouse. Their older brother set about erecting a basketball goal and teaching his siblings how to play baseball and ride a pony. They had pillow fights and water fights. They asked for hammers and nails, shovels and ladders to build things. They put up a tire swing on a limb in the old walnut tree out back.

They found ant hills to study, and snakes, grasshoppers and humming-birds that they might never have seen had they stayed inside watching T.V. all day. They made up stories and developed imaginary characters. The two younger boys started their own make-believe radio and T.V. station in their room upstairs. They interviewed other family members, then wrote and delivered recorded newscasts and sports reports about events concerning our family and others in the community.

Our daughter, Andrea, later recalled that the summer her mother turned off the T.V. was the summer she came to love reading. Since then she has read enough books to fill a small library. She is a singer and song-writer; a lover of literature, theater and language.

Her younger brother, Joe, who founded the make-believe radio and T.V. station, and whose crumpled letter we found in the storage room, had wanted to be president of the United States. That's what he was writing to tell Ronald Reagan when he was nine. He has since settled for being a morning radio personality who does impersonations of politicians and celebrities, and voices of imaginary characters.

The youngest son, Wes, who banged on the old piano and guitar and who played in the dirt with toy soldiers, has become a singer, musician and Marine.

Their oldest brother, Eric, who taught them all how to play ball that summer and who memorized player stats from the backs of his baseball cards, became a sports writer for a newspaper in Evansville, Indiana.

Soon, these children may all have children of their own; new faces and memories to fill more scrapbooks and photo albums as the seasons of their lives pass from spring to fall. One summer, while their children's minds are still fresh and new, I hope they will remember to turn off the T.V.

If You Had the Heart, You Got the Sole

November 1, 1998

THEY aren't much to look at now – the old pair of hightopped Converse All Star white canvas gym shoes that snuggle timidly against each other in the corner of my closet. But they still look great to me.

I felt my feet smiling when they walked past the discarded shoes at a garage sale back in the summer, so I bought them for $2 and for old time's sake.

These shoes could pass for twins of the pair that ran me through high school back in the 1960s. Converse All Star Chuck Taylor models were the Cadillacs of gym shoes in those days – $8.95 a pair, and generally available only to basketball teams.

Otherwise, I would never have considered trying out for basketball. I liked the game just fine and played almost all year on dirt and asphalt courts around home. But I wasn't much good on a gym floor with someone guarding me, and my stocky frame always felt more comfortable in football pads.

Yet I loved Converse All Star Chuck Taylors so much that it made me crazy when the basketball players came strolling by in their new $8.95 shoes. So I signed up for the team and got ready to run my short legs off, if necessary, to get my feet into a pair.

Many other boys apparently had the same idea, because a small army showed up to begin several weeks of fall practice, after which the varsity team would be chosen. That first day we ran wind sprints and shot layups, then ran laps around the gym - up to the tops of the bleachers on each side and back down again, and up and back for a long, long time. We kept running for weeks, until we were no longer boys but just pitiful blobs of sweat and anger, fatigue, soreness and muffled profanities.

In time, many of the boys dropped out, but I did not. The lure of the shoes was too great.

Finally, between fundamental drills, we started running plays and setting defenses. I pretended to be interested, but I was really dreaming of replacing my old worn-out pair of black U.S. Keds with a brand-new pair of white Converse All Stars with Chuck Taylor's autograph on the seal.

I didn't know who Chuck Taylor was but learned years later that he was a guy who may have played semi-pro basketball and who Converse hired in the late 1920s to organize kids' basketball camps for the purpose of selling gym shoes.

Finally the day came when the coaches asked our shoe sizes and told us to bring our $8.95 to the next practice. Several days later, when practice was over, the coach whistled us all together, thanked us for our hard work, passed out our new white canvas Converse All Star Chuck Taylors, and told us he had posted the names of those who had made the varsity team on the wall at the end of the gym.

We crowded around the list, shoving and yelling to see who would dress for the Wildcats that season. What a surprise to see my name wedged between the guy who stood six-feet-four and one who was six-two. I sat down on the bleachers, removed my brand-new white canvas Converse All Star Chuck Taylors from the box, smelled them, laced them up, slipped them on and bounced up and down on the hardwood a few times, just to see if they worked.

Then I found a pencil, marked my name off the roster and left practice for the last time.

Memories for Sale

May 22, 1994

THE favorite porch of my childhood is for sale, complete with a curve at one corner and two sets of steps.

It is attached to an old brick home near the waters of Hanging Fork Creek in Lincoln County, where my great-grandfather, James Harrison Crawford, settled long ago. When I was a boy, my great-aunt Mariah Crawford, an unmarried, retired schoolteacher, lived there alone. Her passions were registered shorthorn cattle and crossword puzzles. She was a small, kindly woman, but I was half-afraid of her. There was an air of sternness about her that whispered she was not to be trifled with.

She lived in one dark little room of the large house. On cold days she sat before the fireplace stirring the embers and poking the logs, reading and working crossword puzzles. But on nice days she worked around the barns or sat on the porch, watching her cattle graze. We lived on neighboring farms, and I was at her house often. It was the first house I ever knew that had its own name – "Xenia Hall."

I loved to stand on the porch and look out upon the world at Aunt Mariah's doorstep. There was a gate between two large maples at the entrance, and a white-gravel lane that crossed a little wooden bridge over a spring-fed branch.

Beside the bridge, at the edge of a pool of water, there grew a patch of mint that perfumed the spot with a perpetual sweet scent. I crawled into the mint patch once and took a long sip of the branch water. It

237

was the best drink of water
I ever had.

Up from the bridge, the
driveway divided at the bottom of a knoll and skirted
some stately cedars to each
side of the house. Many
years ago a four- lane highway took the gate, the trees,
the lane, the bridge and the
mint patch, but it spared the
house and that wonderful
porch to which I was always
drawn when Aunt Mariah's
head was turned.

I wanted to run fast on
the porch, from one end of
it to the other and back, going full-speed in the curve
at the corner. But I didn't
think Aunt Mariah would
approve, so I did it only
when she was out of sight,

My great-grandfather's porch

and even then I ran quietly. I used to peep through the big windows
that faced the porch – into the unused parlor where there were many
books and where an old sword was propped in the corner. I would like
to have played with the sword, but most of all I wanted to bring my
tricycle to Aunt Mariah's and ride on the porch. Sidewalks and paved
driveways were rare in rural Lincoln County in those days, and a long,
smooth wooden porch – with a curve at one corner – seemed an awful
waste of tricycle space.

It took a long time to work up enough nerve to ask, but one day either
I or my parents asked Aunt Mariah if I could ride my tricycle on the
porch, and she politely approved. It must not have been a whole-hearted
endorsement, for I remember riding there only once. But it was one fine
ride. Taking the curve on the tricycle and opening up in the straight-
aways was everything I had imagined, and more.

238

After I saw the "For Sale" sign in front of the place the other day, I stopped and explained to the doctor who now lives there my fondness for the old porch, and asked if I could take a few pictures. He smiled and told me to make myself at home.

The porch had aged a little and has a different wood floor, but its railing and columns are still intact, and its curve at one corner is nearly as charming to me now as it was when I was five years old.

I thanked the doctor for giving me a few minutes with the porch again, and told him I hoped someone with children bought the place – someone with children who ride tricycles.

A Wedding Band
for the Teacher

March 2, 1988

OCCASIONALLY, Rose Hankins still wonders what ever happened to the little boy named George, who was in her first grade class in Louisville in 1929.

Hankins, who was "Miss Slaby" at that time, was a 21-year-old graduate of Louisville Normal School and was living at home with her mother and sisters.

"One morning I was sitting at my desk, going over my lesson plan, and the door opened and George came walking into the room with his fist clenched," she said. "And he walks straight up to me and says, 'Here, I brought you something.'"

The small fist opened and a gold wedding band fell into the teacher's hand.

"I said, 'Why George, this is a nice gift. Where did you get it?'" Hankins recalled.

"Then he started to cry and said, 'Mama and Daddy have been fussing, and Mama took off that ring and threw it at Daddy, and said, 'You take that damn thing! I never want to see it again.' So I picked it up and brought it to you, because you didn't have one.'

"It was heartbreaking," Hankins said. "He was a most unhappy little child. And it broke my heart to see him unhappy."

When the other children arrived and saw George sitting at his desk, sobbing, they wondered what was wrong. "If you've ever been in a classroom of children, the mood of the class can change with whatever is going on," Hankins explained. "I got questions like, 'Did his grandma die? Did his dog run away? Did he lose his lunch money?'"

"Each time I'd say, 'No, George is just unhappy.'"

There was a subdued atmosphere in that room all day long, and the other children would make excuses to go by George and pat him. And each time they'd pat him, he'd cry a little louder. I was a culprit, too. Every time I went by, I patted him too.

At lunch, she said, George wanted nothing to eat, and on the playground at noon recess "he stuck to me like glue."

"When it came time to send the children home, I said, 'George, you wait.' I sat down and wrote a note: 'Dear Mr. and Mrs. —, a broken-hearted little boy sat in my room all day, sobbing and crying. He brought his teacher a present, a wedding ring, because she didn't have one. But I'm returning my gift to you, and I hope it finds its rightful place. Most sincerely, Rose Slaby.'"

"Then I got out my safety pin box ... and I pinned that to him, the ring and the note in an envelope.

"George didn't want to go, but I took him to the front door, and made him promise faithfully that he would go home; kissed him on the forehead, gave him a pat on the back and sent him on his way."

Hankins slept very little that night, worrying over whether she had done the right thing, and about what little George had found when he got home.

"The next day, the door burst open and in comes George like a streak of lightning, throws

PHOTO BY ERIC CRAWFORD

his arms around me, and says, 'It's all right! It's all right!'" she said. "Then he told everything that had happened."

"He said he got home and there they were, looking at each other, mad. He said, 'My Daddy saw the note and read it, and he handed it to Mama, and she read it, and then Daddy took the ring out of the envelope and put it on Mama's finger, and he said, 'That teacher is smarter than we are.'

"I felt like the burden of the world had been lifted from me," Hankins remembered. "My first attempt at being a marriage counselor had been a success."

Although she never heard from George's parents about the incident, any time thereafter that she asked parents to send items from home for class projects, George was the first to bring them in.

Before the school year was over, George and his parents moved out of the city, never to be heard from again. But the teacher, now Mrs. John G. Hankins, 80, of Louisville, has never forgotten the six-year-old boy with tears in his eyes who, nearly 60 years ago, gave her a gold wedding band that he thought no one else wanted.

It was the most touching moment of her 40 years as a first grade teacher.

"I sure would like to see George today," Rose Hankins said. "I'll bet he's a fine person, because he thought of others."

Somewhere, perhaps there is a man named George who feels the same about a teacher that he had in first grade.

Muffins

July 21, 2002

KEVIN Gillespie and Louise Sims couldn't have been a much more unlikely pair of friends when they met a year-and-a-half ago.
He was in his late 20s, married with two small children, and devoting long hours to dental school studies at the University of Louisville near the apartment complex where they both lived on East Chestnut Street.

She was in her mid-80s and lived alone three buildings away, keeping to herself except for moments when she sat on the stairs near a courtyard, crumbling bread and feeding birds.

Louise had grown up in a poor black family in a small town near Nashville, Tenn.; had married young, lost a two-year-old son to pneumonia and had a troubled home life.

Kevin had grown up in a white, middle-class Mormon family in north Salt Lake City, Utah, the second of eight children. His father managed a recycling company and covered Brigham Young University sports for United Press International. His mother ran a day care center.

The friendship between Kevin and Louise blossomed over a plate of freshly-baked raisin muffins. Kevin had been a cook in the military and still loves to bake. One day he asked Louise if she liked muffins, and she replied, "Yes, of course!"

"I told her I had just baked some and would be glad to swing by and drop some off," he said. "From then on we became friends, and I would always make a point of, whenever I would bake something, setting aside a plateful and heading down to Louise's apartment."

The two developed a true friendship during their conversations over Kevin's homemade breads and desserts – which included Louise's favorite, apple pie. Often, Kevin – sometimes with his wife, Megan, and their children, three-year-old Tate and one-year-old Lindsay – would take Louise a plate of food for dinner.

Kevin learned that Louise had no close family ties. She had been living in the apartment for 14 years and, in the beginning, had lived with and cared for her two older sisters. The oldest passed away about seven years ago, and the other sister died two years ago. Louise had used her own life insurance policy to pay for her second sister's funeral.

"There was nothing left for her," Kevin said. "She was very poor and received only a meager Social Security check to live on."

She had no phone, was frail and walked with a cane. As time went on, it took longer and longer for her to answer the door. But even as she grew progressively weaker, she would always assure Kevin, "I'm fine."

One day when she didn't answer the door, he noticed it was unlocked and found her lying on the floor, clutching a lighted flashlight. A table and chair had been knocked over when she fell.

"I propped her head up and gave her some water," Kevin said. "To my astonishment, she said she was fine."

Kevin phoned 911 and later stood by her bedside at Norton Hospital. The next night her waning appetite returned long enough for her to eat the slab of apple pie that he brought from home. He had brought his

schoolbooks to the hospital and he sat by her bed, studying for his up-coming board exams while she rested.

Aside from a chaplain, he was her only visitor.

"During that night she kept looking around and telling me she wanted to go home," Kevin remembered. "I kept telling her she had to get her strength up before she could. She would look at me, take my hand and smile. She slept very peacefully that night."

The hospital phoned the next morning with news that Louise had died.

When Kevin arrived at the hospital, the nurse who had been with Louise when she passed away placed her hand on his shoulder and told him that a nurse who had cared for Louise the night before had told her that, as he was leaving her hospital room that evening, Louise had said, "See that boy that just left? That is the best friend I have ever had."

"She had so very little to give," Kevin said. "But, giving me the best com-pliment I have ever had by calling me friend, she gave me everything."

A Baby's Footprints

July 6, 1994

THERE is an old short story by Sherwood Anderson called "Certain Things Last." It is about certain feelings and scenes – certain small, seemingly forgettable happenings which posterity somehow saves in its scrapbook for each of us until we are old enough to appreciate them.

How and why these delicate episodes in life are not forgotten, while other, more significant ones fade so quickly, must be left to philosophers. But I know that Sherwood Anderson was right. I know that certain things do last. And so does Blanche Reynolds of Los Gatos, Calif. Reynolds was born in Stanford, Ky., in June 1911 to Thomas and Florence Ball. Her father ran a little store on the corner across from the L&N Railroad depot.

When Blanche was still a baby, probably no more than two, a concrete loading dock was poured around the depot, and her father could not resist placing the footprints of his only daughter and youngest child in the wet cement.

He told Blanche later that her left foot made a better impression because she jerked her right foot back from the soft, cool cement before he could press it far enough in to leave a good print.

It was only a moment, on a certain summer day, 81 years ago. But time is nearly always kind to babies' footprints left in cement. And time has taken a special liking to the footprints of Blanche Ball Reynolds – which are still there to this day at the corner of the deserted depot.

PHOTO BY BYRON CRAWFORD

The railroad tracks are gone, grassed over. The depot windows are boarded up, and there are padlocks on its doors. Weeds have grown up through cracks in the concrete. But at the northeast corner of the depot – where a proud father pressed his baby girl's feet into the wet cement – posterity has graciously preserved the moment.

Blanche Reynolds' mother, Florence, died when Blanche was nine. Her father died when Blanche was 17.

"He was a wonderful man," she remembers. "He was loving and caring. I can remember walking with him to see my mother's grave – and the good thoughts he told me, and stories. He was witty, and honest as the day was long. Even after I was a large-sized girl, he always called me 'Baby.' He was in his late 50s when I was born, and I remember him telling me that he had wanted to name me 'Sunshine.' It's a wonder he didn't."

Blanche, a musician, moved to Los Gatos, near San Jose, in 1934, and has been back to Kentucky only once since then, in 1954.

But occasionally some of her relatives here visit the old depot in Stanford just to make sure her baby footprints are still there in concrete, a lasting reminder of a certain tender moment on a certain summer day.

Footnote: The Depot was restored a few years after this story was first published, and the baby's footprints were covered with new concrete. But they remain on this page, true "footnotes."

T-Ball Moments

July 23, 1995

L OST in distant thought on a long, dry highway, I caught only a few words of a story on the car radio.

It was about a little girl on a T-ball team somewhere who had given up a sure home run because she suddenly stopped between third and home plate to pet a dog that had wondered onto the T-ball field.

At last, here was a sports story bigger than its box score; one that did not involve a critical injury or a fight, cheating to win, or poor officiating.

The mental image of the youngster stopping between third and home to speak to man's best friend at the cost of scoring a home run for her T-ball team should be welcomed as a sign that there are still a few kids around who – while they may never be T-ball all-stars – are learning how to run the bases of life.

For a few pleasant moments I thought back to the ball fields where our four children, Eric, Andrea, Joe and Wes, wore their first baggy uniforms.

I still see some of them and their teammates in the outfield, chasing butterflies, pondering an anthill or an earthworm, nearly oblivious to the occasional balls that sometimes bounced their way.

Our family still chuckles about the time our second son, Joe, mystified his coaches and some of the spectators when he began sliding into bases though there was no threat of his being thrown out.

"Why were you doing that?" his mother asked when the game was over.

248

"Well," he said, "the coach patted me on the back and told me to 'go out there and get that uniform dirty.'"

Funny, we all remember that game, but no one remembers the name of the team or anything else about that season. A few short years from now, the same will likely be true for the family of the little girl who gave up the home run to pet the dog.

Kids keep trying to show us what is really important about being a child, but most of us never notice – until it's too late to matter.

The world needs good athletes, I know. And it must have fierce competitors and champions. But in these shockproof days of winning at all cost and survival of the meanest, I like to think there is still room for T-ball players who'd rather stop to pet a dog on the field than to score a homerun, or to slide headfirst into third just to get their uniform dirty.

Footnote: As I am transcribing this story for inclusion in the book, 14 years have passed since its first writing and some of our four children are now parents of their own T-ball players.

One of them, 5-year-old Henry Clay Crawford, was recently spotted by his father, Eric, running the base path with one hand in his pocket.

Later asked why, he sputtered: "Because I didn't want to lose this."

He pulled from his pocket a small toy, plastic police badge.

The tradition continues.

ILLUSTRATION BY WEIDERWOHL

The Best Football Game

November 9, 1997

T HE Monday-morning quarterbacks were huddled around a coffee pot, discussing their most unforgettable football games. I could not help but overhear – and wanted to join them, but didn't.

My most unforgettable game wasn't a game in which I played. In fact I wasn't even there. Almost no one was. But a friend of mine, the wife of one of the referees, was among the handful of people in the stands that mid-October evening in 1980, when two seventh-grade teams tangled on a field behind a school in rural Central Kentucky.

One of the teams was good, the other was bad. So bad that it had not scored a single touchdown the entire season. That was one of four seventh-grade squads organized as part of the feeder system for the county's strong high school football program. The coaches were teachers who had picked their players. Three of the coaches had chosen the best players available. The fourth, a special-education teacher who didn't know much about football, had chosen with his first pick a stocky youngster with a broad smile who answered to the name "Bubba." Because of a birth defect, Bubba had no arms below the elbows.

The coach had never been much of an athlete. One of the painful memories of his childhood, he later told my friend, was that he had always been picked last when playground teams chose sides. Maybe that was why his team of seventh-graders was loaded with kids who might always have been picked last: the boy with no arms, a boy with cerebral palsy and several other youngsters whose strength was confined mostly to the heart.

The other three seventh grade teams were evenly matched, but when one of them played the team coached by the special education teacher, the result was always a rout.

Although the other coaches never seemed satisfied with their teams' winning performances, my friend had noticed all season that the fourth coach would often give high-fives to his losing players who ran fast and got scratched, or even to those who got grass stains or dirt on their uniforms.

Late in that memorable game – with his team down again, maybe 50 or 60 to nothing – the coach called an uncharacteristic timeout. He had decided that Bubba should run the ball, because no one was defending against him.

"Bubba," he instructed, "when they give you the ball, I want you to run like a big dog is after you."

Seconds later, as Bubba clutched the ball between the stubs that were his arms and charged up the middle, it was, my friend said, as though the opposing team was trapped in one of those slow-motion movie sequences reserved for moments magical.

The coach watched with fists clenched against his face as Bubba scampered toward the end zone from about midfield, crossed the goal line, ran between the goal posts, out of the end zone and across the track beyond, stopping only when he reached the fence.

As his teammates embraced their smiling, armless hero and struggled to hoist him into the air for a fitting celebration of their only touchdown of the season, my friend saw the coach sitting on the bench, his face in his hands, crying. She could see his shoulders shaking.

In that splendid little moment, the Rose Bowl, the

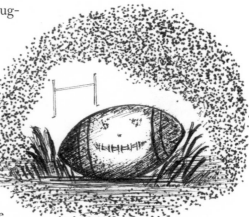

ILLUSTRATION BY B. CRAWFORD

251

Super Bowl and the all-star games could all have been hidden in the exuberant shadows of a ragtag bunch of mostly 12-year-olds, the majority of whom would never play organized football after that season.

One of the referees that night, who would eventually go on to officiate at the college level, later recalled that he had been prepared to throw a crucial block, if necessary, and risk ruining his future as a referee, to see the kid with no arms score the touchdown of his life.

Football has never been quite the same for my friend since that night, or for me since I heard the story five years ago. The Monday-morning quarterbacks may have seen some good games, but they missed the best one.

All Ears for Cheryl

June 17, 1991

S OMEONE at our house taped a Walt Disney anniversary special a while back, and saved for me a segment of the old "Mickey Mouse Club."

Suddenly, as the band played and Mickey led the Mouseketeers in singing "Come along and sing our song and join the jam-bo-ree…" I was swept back to a 1950s-style low-slung easy chair, where I used to curl up and watch the show late every afternoon. Our television was a large, heavy thing with a round, 12-inch screen. We could get only one station, but fortunately it was an NBC affiliate that carried Mickey's gang.

The show was the highlight of my day. It was where I learned to spell e-n-c-y-c-l-o-p-e-d-i-a. I can still sing the "Mickey Mouse March," "The Merry Mouseketeers," "Fun With Music," "Talent Roundup" and "Mousekartoon Time," and I remember that on Wednesday, when Mickey Mouse flew in on a magic carpet to open the show, it was "anything can happen" day. I grew up with Spin and Marty and the Hardy Boys on the Disney Serials, and I was on a first-name basis with all the Mouseketeers.

A few kids had Mickey Mouse Club ears, but my natural ears were large enough to suit me. Besides, it was dangerous in our neighborhood to run around dressed like a large rodent on any day other than Halloween. Although I was way too young to fall in love, and knew it, some of the Mouseketeers were simply irresistible – namely Cheryl and Annette.

Naturally, I was charmed by Annette – the overwhelming heartthrob of most of the club faithful. But as a practical matter, I chose Cheryl to like most. Annette was just a little too pretty for me, and though she smiled at me every day through our big television with the little screen, I knew that on the street in town, she wouldn't have looked twice at me. Cheryl, on the other hand, seemed like a girl who'd stick with me through thick and thin; who would appreciate me just because I was hopelessly devoted to her, and because I liked her an awful lot.

She had a wonderful smile and curly blond locks, and while pretty Annette seemed always in the forefront, Cheryl was usually in the background, dutifully singing and dancing her heart out – just for me.

Sometimes, when the show came to an end – which was about dusk in the winter months – it was all I could do to hold back tears while the camera panned the Mouseketeers' faces as they slowly and sadly sang the goodbye song. "M-I-C... See you real soon... K-E-Y... Why? Because we like you... M-O-U-S-E-EEEEEEE."

Annette would roll her dark eyes toward our tiny television screen, trying her best to woo me, but I waited patiently to catch a fleeting glimpse of Cheryl, way in the back, as the closing march ended and the show faded to black, leaving me alone with only the evening news to ease my pain.

I have seen Annette often over the years on television and in the movies, and she has only improved with age. But I often have wondered what happened to Cheryl, and whether she knew that there was one boy who liked her better than all the rest.

During the Disney anniversary special the other night, I was thinking about her when movie critic Gene Siskel blindsided me with this comment: "I know Annette was the most popular Mouseketeer, but not at my house," he said. "I went for the blonde. I think her name was Cheryl..."

And all these years I thought she was smiling only at me.

Footnote: Cheryl Holdridge died in Santa Monica, California on Jan. 6, 2009 of lung cancer. She was 64.

Louisville's Fourth Street

Date unknown

VEN after all these years without her, sometimes I still miss
Fourth Street.

She was already showing her age and I was just a wet behind
the ears kid from the country when we met in the late 1950s.

Ours was a fleeting, crosswalk kind of romance, but I have never forgotten the way she looked that afternoon, or the words she whispered to
me.

"Young man," she said, "I am the very heart of downtown Louisville.
No matter how many miles may separate us, or how many years before I
see you again, every time you think of this city from this moment on, your
warmest memory will be of me."

She was busy that afternoon. People were crowded around her every corner. Traffic was nearly bumper-to-bumper. Policemen were blowing their whistles, paper boys were yelling, shopping bags rustled. The
mingled sweet scents of fine perfumes and new garments gushed from
the doors of Stewart's, Kaufman's, Bacon's and other elegant department
stores.

Several years later I would take a job in Louisville as a reporter for a
radio station which relocated its studios to Fourth Street. She had lost
some of her charm in the years we'd been apart, but I still thought Fourth
was a sweetheart of a thoroughfare.

During lunch hour I often ambled along her sidewalks, savoring some

255

Christmas 1939, Fourth Street

of the familiar sights, sounds and scents that had first captivated me as a kid. There was a small steakhouse near the Broadway end of Fourth that flame-broiled steaks on a grill in the large front window. I consumed enough red meat there to supply my cholesterol needs well into retirement. But the steakhouse, like the Fourth Street I knew, is long gone.

George Yater, a history buff and the author of "Two-Hundred Years at the Falls of the Ohio," strolled with me one recent afternoon up the street whose name was changed some years ago to the River City Mall. Later it was changed to Fourth Avenue, and last year it was changed back to Fourth Street, as though there must have been magic in the name.

Yater and I reminisced about the street that stole his heart during the 1930s and mine in the 1950s. Yater lived in the South End and would ride the street car downtown with his mother to make the rounds of the stores and to pay bills. They often went to Stewart's, Bacon's Kaufman-Strauss and Jefferson Dry Goods. Yater remembers that on the top floor of Bacon's, directly beneath the large round skylight, encircled by iron railings, were holes in the floor the same size as the skylight. The holes went all the way to the first floor. He liked to drop small slips of paper into a hole on the top floor and watch them flutter to the bottom.

He was intrigued by the toy trains on the second floor of Sutcliffe's Sporting Goods. And he liked to watch the window display decorators in their "soft slippers" arranging mannequins in the store windows.

Years later, after Yater went off to World War II, his parents sometimes sent him newspapers. Once he remembers opening The Courier-Journal Sunday Magazine and seeing an old photo of Fourth Street. "I nearly cried," he said.

In 1972, when Fourth Street was turned into a pedestrian mall, I was living in another city. When I came back to Louisville, Fourth Street was gone and so were most of the businesses and bright lights that had made her sparkle. But she had been right years earlier when she whispered to me that I would never forget her, and every so often I walk past the place where we first met, hoping that perhaps she will have left me a sign that she isn't gone forever.

Footnote: The Courier-Journal photo with this story of a busy sidewalk scene on Fourth Street in 1939 predates my own memories by more than two decades, but offered a great view of Fourth Street in its heyday.

On Writing

February 27, 2000

THE late Red Smith said that writing is easy: "All you do is sit down at a typewriter and open a vein."

We who make a living at this trade often begin to bypass Smith's procedure after battling deadlines for several years. Eventually, some of us let our fingers do all the talking and forget our veins completely.

I have been lucky in this regard. Always, when I stray from the Red Smith method, someone offers a gentle reminder that the source of good writing is the heart.

The latest was Louisvillian Dave Boyle, a husky, smiling man of 80, who shook my hand after a program for veterans in Louisville several weeks ago. We exchanged greetings in a matter of seconds and went our separate ways.

I had nearly forgotten his name when his note arrived a few weeks later, thanking me for taking part in the program and offering a few personal sentiments that he had written in unsteady longhand and that a friend had printed out on a computer. These few words, he said, were the only creative writing he had ever attempted:

Thoughts of a Man of 80
I cannot sing,
I cannot dance,
nor can I write a note,

or play an instrument,
And yet –
My heart is filled with music!
October 1999, Dave Boyle

In his letter, Boyle explained that he had never cared much for poetry, except that of Ogden Nash, and he certainly did not consider himself a poet. He had spent his life in the insurance business. Now, his hands did not work as well as they once did and he apologized for his "scribbling." But he had lost his wife, Hattye Rose, in the spring of 1998, and he had needed to write some thoughts about her. He wanted to share them with me.

I looked over the few lines which he had composed and remembered Red Smith's admonition as I pictured Dave Boyle struggling to make his hand write what his heart was feeling.

"When my wife was diagnosed with cancer my whole life changed. There is nothing of importance in life except human relationships, especially family.

"I wish I had loved her better ..."

"Knowing what my wife and my mother went through, I believe they are already upstairs. When my time comes, I hope to grab a hand from each and pull. If my kids will all push, maybe I'll have a chance."

Over the years I have saved scores of such writings; bits of wisdom, truth and wit that were sent to me, as though keeping them nearby might somehow enrich my own writing.

There is a small, eloquent collection of poems called "Tree People," by John Engle Jr., of Morgan County, who sent me his book knowing that I too love trees and rarely miss the chance to write about them.

Engle speaks of how he learned the language of the leaves before he learned the complex words of men, and of how his spirit finds a fellowship in trees. He remembers when, as a child, he tried to catch sunbeams in a butterfly net, and foolishly believed that he could reach the moon by climbing first a hill and then a tree.

And yet, today I chase the tail of time,
bind up the rushing days
in cords of ink,
cling fast to the invisible hand of beauty,
and try to hold love captive in a word.

Kentucky's Oldest Ham?

August 27, 2006

ET them go moon-eyed over the $500,000 Kentucky State Fair Grand Champion Country Ham if they must. It is only a flash in the pan compared with Kentucky's supposed oldest country ham, of which I serve as humble guardian.

You see, next year there will be a glorious new champion ham, fawned over for a fleeting moment by the media and the hungry. Then it will be drowned in red-eye gravy, smothered in biscuits, crushed among molars of the wealthy and swept away on a tidal surge of steaming coffee.

Kentucky's oldest ham, meanwhile, will remain with us, rock solid and resting easy among other antiquities in my garage. Yes, this is a ham for the ages; a ham with a history.

But is it really the oldest in the state? Well, Sotheby's appraisers have yet to confirm it, but do you know of a country ham older than 42 years?

Its provenance reads like a Kentucky Ham Atlas. Everette Dunagan, for half a century the owner of Dunagan's Grocery & Supply in the rustic Wayne County village of Mill Springs, bought the ham in 1964 from a ham producer in Murray.

"They used to come through the country selling hams," Dunagan told me back in 1984, on the ham's 20th anniversary. "It just weighed nine pounds when I got it, and I put it in a plastic bag, which was a mistake."

After the ham turned dark, Dunagan said he left it hanging with other country hams from the ceiling above the meat counter, and though tourists who stopped by the store near Lake Cumberland often admired the old ham, no one ever bought it. So it just kept growing older and shrinking a few ounces each year. By 1979 it was down to six pounds.

Dunagan claimed that, as most other country hams were going through what are known as "the June sweats," his old ham got down to only two or three drops of grease per summer, and eventually, only one.

It now weighs just over five-and-a-half pounds, and would feel more comfortable wearing an Ace bandage than a blue ribbon.

PHOTO BY BYRON CRAWFORD

This ham dates to the early 1960s

In the summer of 2002, when health problems forced Dunagan, then 76, to sell the store and its inventory, he phoned to say that he wanted me to have the old ham to be kept more or less as a public trust. It still has the loop of baling wire through the shank on which it was suspended for 38 of its 42 years from a hook in the ceiling of Dunagan's Grocery.

Now, it rests in a cozy cardboard box on a shelf in my garage, right next to the antique flour sifter that once was used to create biscuits for long-ago breakfasts.

One year I promised my wife's family that I would bring a country ham for their reunion in Lexington. The cardboard box with the old ham inside had barely landed on the picnic table when the husband of one of my wife's cousins was overcome by curiosity and his appetite.

What price can you put on a Kentucky ham? To First Southern Bank, this year's champion ham was worth $500,000 for charity. But to me, the look on my cousin-in-law's face when he popped the top on the box containing the oldest ham in Kentucky was priceless.

The Gem Supply

December 25, 2005

IF the showcase window of what once was the old Gem Supply Store has survived in downtown Danville from when I was a kid, you might notice that it has a permanent smudge about three feet above the sidewalk.

That's where my nose was pressed against the glass every Christmas as I watched electric trains chase around the maze of tracks.

The Gem was a small but enchanted place, filled floor to ceiling with all kinds of neat toys and sporting goods, bubbling aquariums and exotic fish. During Christmas its sparkle perfectly matched its name.

Inside, there were still more trains whistling past miniature crossings and vanishing into dark tunnels. Young hearts thumped in cadence with the clickety-clack of tiny wheels on rails as children wandered the aisles, lost in the mystical no man's land between fantasy and reality.

My imagination did not need jump-starting in those days. It ran at full throttle all of my waking hours and often in my sleep. Sometimes I dreamed that I worked at the Gem Supply.

The inventory of the Central Kentucky store, coupled with careful searches of the toy pages in the Western Auto, Sears and Montgomery Ward Christmas catalogs, helped me compile my annual letter to Santa Claus.

Santa wrote back only once – a hand-scribbled note beside the plate of crumbs and the empty glass where I had left cookies and milk for him under the tree.

That Christmas I had asked him for a "football suit."

Surely there were other toys I had wanted as well, but the football suit is the only one I remember. It had been love at first sight when I saw it in a Christmas catalog. The color didn't matter much. I could imagine it was any team I liked.

In those days, I was so fast that I often played quarterback and receiver at the same time in the side yard – a virtual one-man show – if no one else was around.

After taking a snap from an imaginary center and faking a hand off, I would loft the pigskin high into the air on a downfield spiral and provide the crowd noise and play-by-play myself, while racing toward the end zone beyond the lilac bush to make a last-second fingertip catch.

In the radiant glow of the big blue, red and yellow lights that filtered through the angel hair in the pre-dawn that Christmas morning, I found a cowboy hat and fringed vest, kerchief and chaps where I had expected to find a helmet, jersey and shoulder pads. My mother discovered the note.

"Dear Byron," it said. "I am sorry that I ran out of football suits this Christmas before I got to your house. I hope you will enjoy this cowboy suit just as much. Thank you for the delicious milk and cookies. Merry Christmas, Old Santa."

I was disappointed with the cowboy suit. Heck, I had already worn out two or three stick horses and enough cap pistols to have defended the Alamo – I was ready for some football!

ILLUSTRATION BY WIEDERWOHL

But my brief disappointment melted away in the excitement of the rare memento that I held in my quivering, peppermint-stained fingers: a personalized, hand-written note, from Santa Claus himself! And in the big soft cushion of the chair where he had sat to have his cookies and milk, there was the honest-to-goodness imprint of the jolly old elf's backside. I was, indeed, favored among children this Christmas morning.

I showed the letter to all my friends. A few doubted the signature's legitimacy, but I knew it was real. Why, I would rather have questioned my own father's signature than to question that of Santa Claus.

Somewhere over the years, both the cowboy suit and that wonderful note have been stolen by time. The cowboy suit alone would be something of value today. But the personalized note to me from Santa Claus would be a treasure.

Regrets

July 1, 2005

I HAVE missed some golden opportunities in my life – far too many to list in this brief space.

Today I am remembering and regretting one in particular: Dr. Thomas Clark's invitation in April 2004 to spend a day with him at his place in the hills of Estill County.

"I come home a different man every time I go in those woods," he said. "Come by here sometime and we'll go. It will be a joy."

Clark, state historian laureate and teacher, died Tuesday just a couple of weeks short of his 102nd birthday.

Last year, we had finished an interview for my column about an endowment that Clark was creating for Lindsey Wilson College through the sale of more than two dozen handsome wooden chests that he had made in the shop at his home in Lexington over the past 50 years, mostly from hardwoods that he had selected from his land.

After the interview, we drifted into conversation about Kentucky's fields and forests. I left the tape recorder running.

"Do you walk in the woods now?" he asked.

"Yes," I told him, "every chance I get."

"My knees are giving out, and I miss it terribly," he said. "I can drive my old truck around through the woods, but I can't walk."

"I do love the woods."

There were times, I consoled him, when I could experience more just by sitting on a log beside the river than I could by walking through the woods on the small place that I own at the foot of a bluff in Anderson County.

He quietly agreed, but I knew that he was not one to enjoy sitting on a log when there was a new path to be taken.

"I have a good bit of this old, worn-out mountain land," he said. "I was up in the woods the other day, and it was a joy to see how well the timber has done; how the land has recovered itself. I do love the woods."

Clark knew about timber. He had grown up on a Mississippi cotton plantation but had come to love the forest while working in the woods as a teenager, and later as a tree farmer.

"One could not stand by and see the great virginal yellow pine sentinels come tumbling down to let the sunshine strike the ground in the scope of their limb spread for the first time in a century and a half, without some emotion," he wrote.

PHOTO COURTESY OF LORETTA CLARK.

If he had not chosen the path of history, Thomas Clark might have become one of America's great woodsmen and conservationists.

As much as I admired him for his genius as a scholar and teacher – and for his ability to see beyond Kentucky's most profound failings to her greatest potential – I came to appreciate him most simply because of his love of trees, which he was still planting when he was 100.

He helped plant a blue ash on his 100th birthday on the grounds of the Kentucky Department for Libraries and Archives in Frankfort. The department is one of many state institutions that are part of a wonderful legacy of a wise man who never stopped giving to us, never stopped teaching us and never stopped believing in us.

If I had it to do it over, I would have taken that day off last year to climb inside Dr. Clark's old truck and ride with him through the green hills of Estill County in the woods that he loved so much – and just listen.

It would have been a joy.

My Parents' Gold Mines

November 8, 1993

M Y dad was never much for gift-giving. It wasn't the money so much, he always said, he just never knew what to give. Yet, for someone who had such difficulty finding gifts, his have always been among the most memorable gifts in our family over the years.

Long ago he gave my mother a pair of house shoes; one on her birthday, December 22, and the other on Christmas. Maybe he gave her something else really nice that year, or money to buy something she wanted, but the house shoes have never been forgotten.

Then there was the Valentine's Day when he gave her a beautiful picture of a heart-shaped box of candy, an advertisement he had clipped from the newspaper. She announced it to the world, and revels in retelling the story.

On Wednesday, my parents, Delbert and Lucille, will celebrate their 50th wedding anniversary. Over breakfast with them last week, I asked my dad if he had picked out a gift for her. He squirmed a bit, as I knew he would, then looked nervously at my mother and back down at his plate. We waited for an answer. "I thought we said we didn't want any gifts," he mumbled.

"That was from other people," I said. "Surely you're going to get her something yourself, and remember, this is the *golden* anniversary."

Dad fumbled with his fork, then solemnly turned to my mother. "In 1935," he said, "Joe Hackley and I staked two or three gold claims in New

Mexico. We marked them with little piles of rocks. Our names are written on strips of paper in Prince Albert tobacco cans that we left in the rocks. I'm giving you the gold claims."

His words took us by surprise. Dad's western adventures as a gold prospector in New Mexico were well-known to us, but he rarely speaks of his prospecting days without encouragement, and even then he usually recounts only our favorite stories; such episodes as his getting lost in the mountains and his burro leading him back to camp as darkness fell across the desert. In all these years, he had never mentioned the gold claims, or the mounds of rocks, or the Prince Albert cans.

"Dad"

As a young man, my dad and his friend, Joe, who had studied geology at Harvard, were prospectors near Glenwood, New Mexico. Dad finally grew tired of prospecting after about one year and moved on to Arizona to take a job as a sheepherder on a large ranch. But Joe kept looking for gold. Dad eventually came home to Kentucky and married my mother, but 17 years later, Joe was still out there searching, and my dad later lost track of him.

We talked for a while about the gold claims, and about Joe Hackley and New Mexico. Dad told mom that the rocks and Prince Albert cans that marked the claims might be gone by now, but that there had been a little gold there when he and Joe staked the claims. Maybe, he said, he and my mother could go to New Mexico one day and find the old claims.

"Mom"

It was a golden moment. He smiled into the eyes of the only real treasure he has ever found, and she smiled back; the smile of a woman with a gold mine.

Index

271